D0236387

FOR THE LOVE OF
THE
ARCHERS

FOR THE LOVE OF THE ARCHERS

Copyright © Summersdale Publishers Ltd, 2015

Illustrations © Shutterstock

All rights reserved.

No part of this book may be reproduced by any means, nor transmitted, translated into a machine language, without the written permission of the publisher.

This is a revised and extended edition of *The Archers: An Unofficial Companion* by Rosie Dillon (2011), which contained research by Sarah Herman.

Beth Miller has asserted her right to be identified as the author of this work in accordance with sections 77 and 78 of the Copyright, Designs and Patents Act 1988.

Condition of Sale
This book is sold subject to the condition that it shall not, by way of trade or otherwise, be lent, resold, hired out or otherwise circulated in any form of binding or cover other than that in which it is published and without a similar condition including this condition being imposed on the subsequent purchaser.

Summersdale Publishers Ltd
46 West Street
Chichester
West Sussex
PO19 1RP
UK

www.summersdale.com

Printed and bound in the Czech Republic

ISBN: 978-1-84953-773-5

Substantial discounts on bulk quantities of Summersdale books are available to corporations, professional associations and other organisations. For details contact Nicky Douglas by telephone: +44 (0) 1243 756902, fax: +44 (0) 1243 786300 or email: nicky@summersdale.com.

FOR THE LOVE OF
THE
ARCHERS

AN UNOFFICIAL
COMPANION

BETH MILLER

summersdale

FOREWORD

This detailed little book, *For the Love of The Archers* by Beth Miller, brought back fond memories for me, as I am now in my forty-first year of playing Brian Aldridge. I often find it hard to believe that all that time has passed, since aged 32 (I am five months older than Brian) I joined the *Archers* cast, but in reading and poring over the facts, from its beginning in 1951 to the present day, it is easier for me to come to terms with the passage of time. What a passage of time it has been for the programme, though: the longest running drama series in the world. All of us involved in *The Archers*, in whatever capacity – actors, producers, writers, technical staff – are proud of the part we play.

For the Love of The Archers will bring gasps of joy and horror, amusement and recollection to all, from those aging listeners who boast, quite rightly, to having listened to every episode since its inception, to those who have become addicted more recently. So sit back with a cup of tea, or something stronger, and wallow in this bran tub of *Archers* facts and figures. I did, and I have to confess how little I knew, and how much I had forgotten. This book will really help me now with the continuity, as I continue, hopefully, to play Brian into his dotage!

Charles Collingwood, June 2015

AUTHOR'S NOTE

Unlike Ambridge, which is a constant in an uncertain world, this book does not have a fixed structure. The reader is encouraged to dip in and out, lingering wherever they like. There are, though, some waymarkers in the form of repeating features. For instance, there are brief descriptions of the important locations in the village, under the heading 'Welcome to Ambridge'. Pen portraits of all the main inhabitants are offered in 'Meet the Characters', while those who have shuffled off this mortal radio coil are commemorated in 'Gone But Not Forgotten'. 'Famous Faces in Ambridge' details the celebrity appearances in radio's favourite village, while 'Making *The Archers*' offers fascinating glimpses behind the scenes. Some of the themes that have cropped up in the programme are explored in 'Issues in Ambridge', and *Archers* fans, well-known and not, share their loves and hates in the 'Listener Portraits' which are sprinkled throughout the book. Some key storylines are relived in 'Memorable Moments', and you can test your in-depth knowledge by heading along to 'Quiz Night at the Bull' (answers at the back of the book). There are also a few stand-alone sections, to keep you on your toes. However you read the book – page by page, section by section, or from the back – and whether you are a hardcore fanatic or a brand-new listener, I hope it enhances your appreciation of all things Ambridge.

CONTENTS

MEET THE CHARACTERS

PORTRAIT OF THE WRITER
AS A LISTENER:

MAKING THE ARCHERS

MEMORABLE MOMENTS

NOT FROM ROUND 'ERE

OH, SO QUIET!

QUIZ NIGHT AT THE BULL

VILLAGE FÊTE

VILLAGE PRODUCTIONS

WELCOME TO AMBRIDGE

INTRODUCTION

'Well, me old pal, me old beauty,' were the soon-to-be legendary words that Walter Gabriel chortled on Whit Monday, 29 May 1950. As the programme began its five-day pilot run, the now familiar tune of 'Barwick Green' introduced the Midlands to the Archer family and the minutiae of their rural lives. Over sixty-five years later, *The Archers* is the longest-running drama serial of all time, anywhere in the world, and continues to draw almost five million listeners every week in the UK alone.

While it just recounts the lives of ordinary country folk from Ambridge, this hasn't stopped fans tuning in for five or, in recent years, six episodes every week to keep up to date with their favourite farmers. From dramatic births and deaths, love affairs and violent crimes to foot-and-mouth, farm sales, business ventures, cricket matches and village fêtes, Ambridge life is anything but dull. The commitment to lengthy storylines and the longevity of families and characters makes the programme's depiction of rural life realistic, but also entertaining and often gripping and moving for listeners.

But mainly it's the humdrum everyday life of the Ambridge villagers that keeps us coming back for more. For many fans 7 p.m. just wouldn't be the same without a drink at The Bull, a chat in the kitchen at Brookfield Farm or the gentle moo of a cow grazing on open pasture. And who could imagine summer without the stalls of the village fête, September without knowing who's grown the best beans for the Flower and Produce Show and the build-up to Christmas without Lynda Snell plotting another theatrical extravaganza?

Covering the farms, families, deaths, dramas, animals and community antics, this book is a trip down a country memory lane and a delightful compendium of facts and frolics of *Archers* life. Find out what goes on behind the scenes and test your knowledge of Britain's best-loved radio drama with the themed quizzes throughout the book. Now, raise a pint of Shires to many more years of Ambridge.

HOW IT ALL BEGAN

In the first five pilot episodes of *The Archers*, which aired in just the Midlands in Whit Week, 1950, the Archer family worked on Wimberton Farm, on the fringe of the village of Ambridge. Wimberton Farm was changed to Brookfield Farm for the three-month trial run, broadcast nationally from 1 January 1951.

The original idea for the programme came from well-known Lincolnshire farmer Henry Burtt at a meeting between the BBC and farming representatives when he announced, 'What we need is a farming *Dick Barton*.' *Dick Barton* was an adventure serial surrounding the exploits of a secret agent.

Up until 1962, almost every one of the 3,000 *Archers* episodes was written by *Dick Barton* scriptwriters Geoffrey Webb or Edward J. Mason.

The programme was originally made for £47 per episode.

The first editor Godfrey Baseley used to invite senior figures from the farming world to appear as themselves on the programme. In 1961 Sir Richard Trehane, chairman of the Milk Marketing Board, visited Ambridge and stayed as a guest of Charles Grenville and Carol Grey.

Originally, cast members were paid varying amounts due to budget constraints – between £9 and £12 a week – but to avoid disputes they were led to believe they were all receiving the same fee. This wasn't kept a secret for long and Norman Painting (Phil Archer) was quick to voice his complaints when he discovered he was earning £2 less each week than Harry Oakes (Dan Archer).

An introductory programme to ease listeners into *The Archers* before it started airing nationally was produced by Godfrey Baseley and transmitted in December 1950. The programme featured Godfrey visiting 'Ambridge' in a 'mobile recording vehicle' and talking to the characters as if they were real. He had a cup of tea at Brookfield Farm and commented on the possibility of a romance between Phil and Grace. The programme ended with Godfrey inviting listeners to come and eavesdrop some more on these country folk in January 1951.

Within weeks of the first national episodes airing, the programme had an audience of two million.

Representatives from the Ministry of Agriculture and Fisheries (now the Department for Environment, Food and Rural Affairs) and the National Farmers' Union were on the programme's original advisory team, helping writers to include factual and informative farming messages.

WELCOME TO AMBRIDGE: AMBRIDGE HALL

- Ambridge Hall was originally built as the home for the village doctor.
- Erected in the 1860s, the Hall is built from yellow brick, has six bedrooms and a garden that extends down to the River Am.
- Laura Archer originally left Ambridge Hall to her lodger Colonel Danby in her will, but never signed the top copy of the will, so it was sold off to the Snells.
- The Snells decided to transform their home into a guest house, decorated – naturally – using the principles of feng shui.
- Lynda Snell developed the gardens so they were full of low-allergen plants, including a Shakespearean plot that only features plants named in the works of the Bard, in a possibly unconscious but wholly appropriate homage to E. F. Benson's novel *Mapp and Lucia* (1931). Lynda was delighted when Matthew Wilson visited the garden to record a special feature for *Gardeners' Question Time* in early 2011.

�֍ Unfortunately, the house and garden, being right on the Am, were submerged in the dramatic floods of 2015. Lynda's delightful garden was sadly ruined, and the Hall left in need of some serious redecorating. However, these material losses were as nothing compared to the disappearance of Scruff, the Snell's beloved dog, now presumed dead.

ISSUES IN AMBRIDGE:
ORGANIC vs GM

On 2 April 1984 milk quotas were introduced into the EU for farms producing milk or other milk products to try to restrain the rise in milk production. In Ambridge this saw Brookfield Farm reduce its dairy herd from 110 to 95 to comply with the quota it was set. The milk quotas gave Tony and Pat Archer the incentive they needed to turn Bridge Farm organic. By reducing their dairy herd they were able to let go their full-time worker Malcolm Lewis and dedicate more funds and time to cutting out artificial fertilisers, herbicides and pesticides. They made a commitment to converting 30 acres a year over five years and in 1985 they grew 10 acres of organic wheat, carrots and potatoes. By 1989 they were able to declare themselves fully organic and apply for Soil Association status. The storyline was inspired by a scriptwriter's visit to Brynllys Farm in Ceredigion, Wales, the UK's first certified organic dairy farm.

When Brian Aldridge received hefty subsidy cheques for Home Farm in the 1990s, Tony and Pat were jealous – subsidies for organic farmers were considerably less – but proud of their achievements. Yet in 1999 their younger son Tom was so outraged by the introduction of GM oil seed rape on Brian's land that he destroyed the crop and faced criminal charges. This was a realistic reflection of the disputes between organic and GM producers going on in the countryside. Two years after Tony Blair's 1997 electoral promise to introduce licences for experimental farming and reduce anti-GM hysteria, producers and consumers were still battling it out. While some farmers embraced GM crops and regarded dissenters as 'anti-science', organic farmers were concerned that modified organisms would cross-pollinate with natural species, changing them irreversibly for the future.

There was no denying the success of organic farming, with sales of organic products in the UK increasing from £100 million in 1993/94 to £1.21 billion in 2004 (and to £1.86 billion in 2014). Bridge Farm reflected this growth as Pat expanded her dairy business from yogurt to ice cream and secured a lucrative contract with Underwoods, the Borchester department store. In 2000 the Archers opened their own farm shop in Borchester, 'Ambridge Organics', selling daughter Helen's well-known cheeses among the array of other organic offerings. But in 2011 the organic dream became more of a nightmare, as an outbreak of *E. coli* was traced back to Bridge Farm ice-cream. The fallout, during which the accidental culprit Clarrie resigned, left the farm's reputation – and income – in tatters. Rebranding the ice cream from Bridge Farm to Ambridge Organics helped somewhat, but the business struggled to regain its former status. Tom eventually convinced Tony and Pat to sell the dairy herd and buy in milk from elsewhere to make their products. In 2015 Helen and Tom made the decision to sell their shop in Borchester, following poor sales, and relocate it back to Bridge Farm, where there had originally been a farm shop in the 1990s.

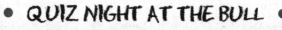

WHAT'S ON IN AMBRIDGE?

1. Which Ambridge event is celebrated on or around 21 October?

2. Where did the fireworks take place to mark the Queen's Coronation in 1953?

3. In 2003 which event saw the residents of Ambridge raise £300 for the church?

4. What was the name of the original donkey used at Ambridge's Palm Sunday services before Benjamin took his place?

5. What was the theme of Valentine's Night at The Bull in 2015?

6. Which popular literary character did Daniel Hebden Lloyd dress up as for Halloween in 2001?

7. Who co-produced 2003's Ambridge Mystery Plays with Lynda Snell?

8. At which event is the Lawson-Hope Cup presented?

9. Who was crowned Miss Ambridge at the 1977 Ambridge Fête, despite being from Penny Hassett?

10. In which country did Bert and Freda Fry spend Valentine's Day in 2006?

11. What was planted in 2012 to celebrate the Queen's Diamond Jubilee?

12. What potentially dangerous incident was narrowly averted at Brookfield's Open Farm Sunday in 2012?

MEET THE CHARACTERS:
THE ARCHERS OF BROOKFIELD FARM

David and Ruth live and work at Brookfield, which was inherited from David's father Phil. David's mother Jill now lives with them, along with their children Pip, Josh and Ben. Pip's beginning to forge her own career in farming, while Josh and Ben are still at school, though Josh is keen on farming and is likely to join the family business one day. Jill cooks up a storm, keeps bees and still misses Phil, to whom she was married for more than fifty years. David usually seems to be estranged from one of his siblings: most recently Kenton, after David backed out of selling Brookfield; and Elizabeth before that, because of what she regarded as David's role in her husband Nigel's death.

In 2014 Ruth was the driving force behind a planned move to Prudhoe, where her ailing mother lives. The family came close to moving, making an offer on a farm in Northumberland, and accepting Justin Elliott's over-the-odds offer of £7 million for theirs. But David couldn't go through with the plan and backed out, so it looks like there will be Archers at Brookfield for a long time to come.

David and Ruth's marriage has been rocked by infidelity, breast cancer, a miscarriage, and a complete difference of opinion about leaving Ambridge. But it seems to always continue, strong as ever.

DID YOU KNOW?

✁ Jill was wearing a yellow dress when Phil spotted her for the first time at the fête in 1957.

✂ Phil served as a JP on the Borchester Bench and was chairman of the local NFU.

✂ Jill and Phil named their twins Shula and Kenton by throwing alphabet blocks into the air.

✂ David Archer failed his mathematics A Level twice.

✂ Ruth did not promise to 'obey' David in her marriage vows made in 1988.

✂ Philippa Rose Archer, known by all as Pip, was named after her granddad Phil and her Aunt Rose.

✂ Joshua Matthew Archer is, like his older sister Pip, a natural farmer. Jill taught him the skills of bee-keeping.

✂ Benjamin David Archer was born at home at Brookfield Farm on Eddie Grundy's birthday.

✂ Whatever else David does, he will most likely be remembered for the time he shot a badger in a fit of rage.

PORTRAIT OF THE WRITER AS A LISTENER:
JOANNA TROLLOPE

Joanna Trollope is the best-selling author of seventeen novels, including A Village Affair, The Rector's Wife *and* The Choir.

When and why did you start listening? It's been so long that I can't remember how or why I started – possibly because I'm old enough to remember *Mrs Dale's Diary*, and I think *The Archers* must have been a natural follow on!

What's your most memorable Ambridge moment? I thought the scene where Elizabeth confessed her fling with Roy to her mother was wonderfully well acted and written. I always think *The Archers* are at their best for scenes of emotional crisis – those are as good as the attempts at broad comedy are cringeworthy.

Which character would you most like to meet? One of the subtler characters – someone like Usha, for example.

Which character drives you crazy? The ones who drive me crazy, with the exception of Clarrie, are the Grundys...

If you could make one change to *The Archers*, it would be... The one change I would like to make is the sort of Mummerset treatment of all the people with regional accents – but I think its general narrative and emotional drive is wonderful!

WELCOME TO AMBRIDGE: ARKWRIGHT HALL

- The Hall is situated in Grey Gables Country Park by its own lake.
- While the house is Victorian, its foundations date back as early as the seventeenth century.
- After Charles Grenville bought the building in 1959, John Tregorran supervised its renovation and saw it transformed into a community centre.
- Before Jack Woolley became the Hall's new owner in 1965, the youth-orientated Cellar Club (opened in 1963) provided a soundproofed room for bands to play and kept the building in use.
- The Hall has been a leisure centre and a field studies centre, but was left unoccupied for many years. It has since been renovated by the Landmark Trust and serves as distinctive holiday accommodation.

RIP

GONE BUT NOT FORGOTTEN:
MARK HEBDEN

Born: 20 February 1955
Died: 17 February 1994
Played by: Richard Derrington

If any Ambridge couple could be said to have taken their time to 'get it together', Mark Hebden and Shula Archer would be in line for the title. Despite proposing to her on New Year's Eve 1980, Mark didn't tie the knot with Shula until nearly five years later, and even then married life was hardly a smooth ride. While Mark was a good egg – Borchester Under-14 Judo Champion, hang-gliding and sky-diving enthusiast and passionate solicitor with promising career prospects – it took Shula some time to figure out he was the man for her. In the interim, Mark embarked on relationships with Jackie Woodstock (she proposed, but he ended it over accusations she was flirting with other men on a skiing holiday) who lived with him at Penny Hassett, and fiancée Sarah Locke – the blonde, bubbly daughter of the senior partner at law firm Locke and Martin. When that engagement went south, Mark took a job offer in Hong Kong to help him move on. Shula visited him there and on his return he proposed to her on Lakey Hill.

Unfortunately, their married life was no smoother than their courtship. They struggled to conceive a baby – Shula had an ectopic pregnancy, and eventually after battling her demons over her sister's abortion, they opted for IVF – and Mark's commitment to his work put a lot of strain on the relationship. After a stint working in Birmingham he moved a lot closer to home, setting up a practice in Borchester with Usha Franks (then Gupta) as his partner. Before his death he took on the controversial case of defending Susan

Carter when she was accused of hiding her fugitive brother Clive. Tragically, Mark never did learn the wonderful news that his wife's second shot at IVF had been successful. On 17 February 1994, a few days shy of his thirty-ninth birthday, Mark was driving home when a reckless driver overtook him on a blind bend – he swerved to avoid horse rider Caroline Bone, whose horse had thrown her to the ground, and ploughed into a tree. He died instantly and missed the birth of his longed-for son Daniel and what could have been many happy years together with Shula. He is commemorated every year with the Single Wicket Competition, the winner of which is awarded the Mark Hebden Memorial Trophy.

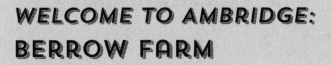

WELCOME TO AMBRIDGE: BERROW FARM

- Despite its bucolic name, this 'mega-dairy' is home to 1,500 cows and uses the highest of high-tech. The plan for the dairy was originally proposed by Debbie Aldridge, and championed by her stepfather Brian, though it's been run by Damara Capital since their takeover of Borchester Land in 2014.
- Brian's backing of the controversial farm caused friction with some members of his immediate family, particularly Adam, and his brother and sister-in-law Tony and Pat, who were horrified at the thought of cattle being kept permanently indoors.
- Rob Titchener was brought in as herd manager in January 2013.
- The fact that the cows' slurry would be used to supply an anaerobic digester appalled quite a lot of other village folk, particularly those living downwind of Berrow Farm. There were public meetings and demonstrations against the building of the farm, but it went ahead anyway, with the first heifers arriving in August 2013.
- At the Open Farm Sunday in 2014, a cow went into labour, but unfortunately the calf died, which was of course the image that the local paper ran with.

FAMOUS FACES IN AMBRIDGE: PART 1

It may be a small rural community nestled near the Hassett Hills, but that hasn't stopped some big names from popping round for a visit. In fact a number of well-known faces – or rather, voices – have appeared as themselves on the programme over the last sixty years, mingling with the good country folk of Ambridge.

★ The annual fête in 1952, held on the last Saturday in June, was opened by **Gilbert Harding**. The journalist and *What's My Line?* panellist had worked with *Archers* creator Godfrey Baseley on some of his earlier farming programmes.

★ Band leader **Humphrey Lyttelton** showed up in Ambridge in 1957 to open the church fête to raise money for the roof. The humorous jazz musician delivered a speech poking fun at the vicar and his 'outlaws' trying to take money from the rich to help the poor church roof!

★ After Dan Archer bumped into World War Two army veteran and *Dam Busters* actor **Richard Todd** at a National Dairy Farmers' lunch, he persuaded him to stop by the village to open the 1962 village fête. Much to 17-year-old Jennifer Archer's delight, her grandfather invited the actor for a drink at The Bull, even if she did have to listen to them talking about farming.

★ Ambridge hosted its first royal visit in 1984 when **Princess Margaret** made an appearance as herself. She was attending the Borsetshire NSPCC Centenary Fashion Show held at Grey Gables – the charity of which she was president. Her part was recorded at Kensington Palace, where the Princess was concerned about noise being made by plumbers and the sound of a ticking clock in the room.

★ When Robert and Lynda Snell went to see **Dame Edna Everage** at the theatre in 1988 they found themselves sitting so close to the front that Lynda found herself being addressed by Dame Edna herself and becoming the butt of some of Edna's jokes, although Lynda thought it was in fact *she* who had upstaged the international comedienne. The scene was recorded in the Birmingham Hippodrome in front of the real audience of the programme and most of what was said was improvised.

WELCOME TO AMBRIDGE:

BLOSSOM HILL COTTAGE

- This idyllic cottage is situated on a side road off the Borchester Road, making it slightly removed from the rest of the village.
- It's been owned by Mike Daly, John Tregorran, Ralph and Lilian Bellamy, Peggy Archer and current owner Usha Franks. It's now rented out to Helen Archer, who lives there with her son Henry and her fiancé Rob.
- The two-bedroom house was used by Kate Aldridge and her gang of teenage friends to hang out.
- It's survived a burglary, a fire and an attack by racist vandals who sprayed offensive graffiti, targeted at Usha Franks (then Gupta), on its walls in 1995.

QUIZ NIGHT AT THE BULL

BITES AND PIECES

1. On what day of the week is the twice-monthly Borchester Farmers' Market held?

2. Whose stag night took place on Shrove Tuesday in 1994?

3. In which month of the year does Marmalade Making traditionally take place?

4. Who received a medal from the British Legion for selling remembrance poppies for over thirty years?

5. Who hosted a ghost walk that began at The Bull in 2008?

6. What variety of apple, bought from a supermarket, stumped Lynda Snell in an identification contest on 2005's Apple Day?

7. Who challenged Alistair to the Three Peaks Challenge in 2003?

8. Tom Forrest formed the Ambridge branch of a shooting club in 1953 to hunt which animal?

9. Who was the WI's representative at the National Energy Conference in 1978?

10. In 1994 residents hosted a ceremony to mark the twinning of Ambridge with which village in France?

11. What did John Tregorran leave Jennifer in his will?

12. Who gave a talk titled 'Agriculture in Australia' to the Ambridge WI?

PORTRAIT OF THE PODCASTER AS A LISTENER:
LUCY FREEMAN

Lucy is co-presenter of the Dum Tee Dum podcast, a weekly discussion of goings-on in Ambridge.

When and why did you start listening? 1980, at the age of eight, in our family home in Northamptonshire. My mother was an avid listener and I can still see her loading the twin tub with sheets and saying 'Oh for goodness' sake!' at Eddie, who had suggested something ridiculous to Clarrie.

What's your most memorable Ambridge moment? It ought to be Nigel going off the roof but in actual fact it is Elizabeth being dumped by the side of the road by horrible Cameron Fraser. It was the first time I ever felt I genuinely could not wait for the next episode of something. I was so worried about Elizabeth. I wanted to be a journalist like her and she didn't seem to fit in in the country, and I identified with that.

Which character would you most like to meet? Jim Lloyd. So waspish and funny.

Which character drives you crazy? Kate. She's written to annoy, and it works.

The Archers **is wonderful because...** like all treasures, from P. G. Wodehouse's London to E. F. Benson's Tilling, it is its own self-contained little world, that ticks along happily from season to season. We just open the door to it and they're all there, going about their business.

If you could make one change to *The Archers* it would be... pulling the Christmas show back from the brink of disaster every single year. Just let it be a huge failure, just for one Christmas!

BORSETSHIRE BIRTHDAYS

Do you share a birthday with any of the current crop of Ambridge residents? Check out the dates below.

2 January Henry Archer
7 January Jennifer Aldridge
10 January Pat Archer
16 January Bethany Tucker
21 January Brenda Tucker
30 January Kathy Perks

2 February Roy Tucker
9 February Will Grundy
16 February Tony Archer
17 February Pip Archer
25 February Tom Archer

15 March Ben Archer
15 March Eddie Grundy
30 March James Bellamy

3 April Caroline Sterling
5 April Robert Snell
6 April Keira Grundy
7 April George Grundy
16 April Helen Archer
21 April Elizabeth Pargetter

1 May Hayley Tucker
12 May Clarrie Grundy
22 May Neil Carter
29 May Lynda Snell
16 June Ruth Archer
17 June Usha Franks
19 June Fallon Rogers
22 June Christopher Carter
22 June Adam Macy
28 June Phoebe Aldridge

3 July Abbie Tucker
8 July Lilian Bellamy
20 July Jamie Perks

1 August Johnny ('Rich') Phillips
7 August Matt Crawford
7 August Emma Grundy
8 August Kenton Archer
8 August Shula Hebden Lloyd

13 September Josh Archer
18 September David Archer
18 September Joe Grundy
28 September Ed Grundy
29 September Alice Carter
30 September Kate Madikane
30 September Poppy Grundy

3 October Jill Archer
10 October Susan Carter

9 November Clive Horrobin
11 November Brian Aldridge
13 November Peggy Woolley
14 November Ruairi Donovan
14 November Dan Hebden Lloyd

1 December Mike Tucker
12 December Lily and Freddie Pargetter
21 December Christine Barford
24 December Debbie Aldridge

MEET THE CHARACTERS:
CHARLIE THOMAS AND JUSTIN ELLIOTT

Smooth-talking Charlie works for Justin Elliott, the boss of Damara Capital, as a kind of enforcer. Damara made a hostile takeover of BL (Borchester Land) in 2014, rocking poor Brian's world, and subsequently Charlie was here, there and everywhere as he worked tirelessly to improve profits and yields.

Lower-profile Justin lives in London with wife Miranda, but seemed to be interested in a more rural life when he made an over-the-odds offer for Brookfield.

DID YOU KNOW?

✻ Enigmatic Charlie's sexuality seemed as fluid as a pint of Shires. But when his close lady-friend, Rebecca, turned out to be his sister, he and Adam shared a kiss on New Year's Eve as the clock chimed into 2015, interrupted by an outraged Helen.

✻ When Adam saved Charlie from drowning during a crazy mid-flood attempt to clear a drain, he gave him another kiss, the kiss of life. Adam may prefer to forget that he sobbed, 'Don't leave me,' during this incident.

✻ Justin's keen on game shooting, and organised his own shoot for local farmers.

✻ Charlie is more of a technology man and is never happier than when playing with drones or other new bits of kit.

MAKING THE ARCHERS:
THE VOICES BEHIND
THE VILLAGERS

The creator of *The Archers*, radio producer Godfrey Baseley, insisted on using a mixture of professional actors and 'normal' people in the recording of the programme. He believed that only with this injection of real-life country-dwellers and senior figures from the farming world would the necessary authenticity be achieved. Some of the programme's best-loved personalities emerged from this casting philosophy and have lived a slice of *Archers* life for real. For example, Bob Arnold (who played Tom Forrest) grew up in the Cotswolds, where his own father ran a village pub. He worked as a butcher and painted white lines on the roads of Oxfordshire before appearing in a BBC programme about the Cotswolds, which led to more appearances on BBC Midlands programmes and variety shows where he was known as 'Bob Arnold – The Farmer's Boy'.

Godfrey's philosophy holds less sway nowadays. The present editor of *The Archers*, Sean O'Connor, has talked publicly about his decision to replace some of the younger cast members with older actors who have been professionally trained. This policy has, most notably, brought us a new Tom. The part was originally played by Tom Graham, but after jilting Kirsty at the altar and running off to Canada, he returned in late 2014 with a new voice, that of William Troughton. Pip Archer has also had a rebrand and is now played by the rurally-named Daisy Badger.

With a regular cast of about sixty characters, *The Archers* is by no means a full-time job and even principal cast members only spend a few days a month in the recording studio. Because recording only takes place once every four weeks, and because not all cast members feature in every episode, actors are able to pursue other projects while their character remains on the show, such as appearing in films, TV and stage work. Storylines are often written to accommodate these commitments – Debbie Aldridge runs a farm in Hungary so that when actress Tamsin Greig is not working on shows such as *Episodes* or *Friday Night Dinner* she can pop back to Ambridge so Debbie can catch up with the family.

Another advantage that *The Archers* has over rival TV serial dramas, where its actors are concerned, is that even if cast members decide to leave, or sadly pass away, it doesn't necessarily mean the end of the road for their characters. The actress who played Kate Madikane, Kellie Bright, left to take on the role of Linda Carter in *Eastenders*, and Kate is now voiced by Perdita Avery. Perdita began her career in theatre, and has had roles in TV, including on *Midsomer Murders* and *Hollyoaks*. Kellie and Perdita aren't the only ones to move between Ambridge and a career in film or TV. Lucy Davies, the original Hayley, went on to star in *The Office* and the Simon Pegg movie *Shaun of the Dead*. And Felicity Jones, who used to be Emma Grundy, has been in several films, and was nominated for an Oscar for her role in *The Theory of Everything*.

A number of Ambridge residents have been voiced by multiple actors over the years, perhaps most notably Dan Archer, who made it almost to the age of ninety thanks to the voices of four different men, but also the late John Tregorran, who was voiced by five different actors on the programme. John's widow, Carol, who recently returned to Ambridge, is now played by Eleanor Bron (in a role formerly taken by Anne Cullen). And the original Clarrie Grundy, Heather Bell, is back in the same role she created in 1979. Heather played the part for about seven years, before Fiona Mathieson briefly took over. Then in 1988 Rosalind Adams stepped into Clarrie's wellies, and stayed for more than twenty-five years. When Rosalind retired in 2013, Heather Bell returned once again, to reprise the cry of 'Ohhhh, Eddie!'

WELCOME TO AMBRIDGE: BRIDGE FARM

✂ Bridge Farm is home to Pat and Tony Archer, son Tom Archer and grandson Johnny Phillips. It's an organic farm, which produces yogurt, ice cream and cheese. The farm also has its own pigs and produces a range of vegetable crops.

✂ The family is particularly attached to their red-brick Victorian home on the farm.

✂ Bridge Farm converted to organic in 1984 and Pat and Tony received the coveted Soil Association symbol for their produce a year later.

✂ The farm supplies the Archer family's own shop with their produce, including daughter Helen's Borsetshire Blue cheese. The shop, Ambridge Organics, is currently in Borchester but is likely to move back to the farm.

✂ Pat and Tony's eldest son John died in a tractor accident in one of the farm's fields in 1998. The son that John never knew he had, Johnny, came to live at Bridge Farm in 2014 and works as an apprentice on the farm.

✂ In 2008 Helen and her brother Tom became partners in the business, and they encouraged their parents to buy the freehold of the 140-acre farm, which with the help of a large mortgage the family were able to do.

✂ Tom left his pigs to the tender mercies of his family when he ran away to Canada following his jilting of Kirsty.

✂ After selling the dairy herd, Tony decided to go into beef cattle instead. However, in 2014 he suffered a terrible accident when he was crushed by his prize bull. His injuries meant he was in hospital for many weeks, though he slowly recovered, much to his family's relief. Tom returned after Tony's accident, full of renewed vigour and energy, ready to help get the farm back up and running.

MEMORABLE MOMENTS: TOM JILTING KIRSTY

Date: 24 April 2014
Location: St Stephen's Church

Hearing Tom stumble through his hard-to-comprehend explanations in the vestry was so painful. Did he actually say 'It's not me, it's you' or is that just how we remember it? Then we had to witness poor Kirsty desperately trying to make it right after her Bridezilla antics of the previous weeks: 'We can get married quietly later on!', 'We can forget about the house!', 'We don't even have to get married, we can just live together!' Then, and we wished we could have repressed this, we heard Tom start to cry… We will never forget it, though we might wish we could. We were pinned there, helpless, horrified spectators to Kirsty's justifiable anger – this was, after all, the second time Tom had dumped her – and finally, there was her race out of the church, the rustling of many fluffy white layers of dress, and that final, almighty scream. We would have slept easier had we simply gone from Roy telling Kirsty that Tom wanted to speak to her, to the scream, intercut with a scene about Pat's hat.

Horrified tweeters berated the hapless non-groom: 'Oh Tom, how could you?! Poor Kirsty,' cried @moorhouseb. And, 'Oh my god Tom you are such a coward! How could you be so horrid?!' echoed @LottieLandGirl. Others felt more exasperated than shocked: 'Oh for goodness sakes couldn't we have had a happy wedding without trauma,' @westlynnjersey complained.

QUIZ NIGHT AT THE BULL

CHARMED CHILDHOODS

1. Where was Susan Carter when her daughter Emma started wetting the bed in 1994?

2. When Christine passed her School Certificate what gift did Dan Archer give her to show how proud he was?

3. To get her son Daniel to eat carrots, Shula used to cut them into the shape of which animal?

4. Who was German au pair Eva Lenz hired to look after?

5. Where did Kate hold the naming ceremony for her daughter Phoebe?

6. Which one of Helen Archer's brothers preferred wearing a pair of her trousers than his own when he was six?

7. Which child has the longest name in Ambridge?

8. How old was Joe Grundy when he left school?

9. Who was Clive Horrobin's favourite superhero as a child?

10. Which teenager gave birth to baby Kylie (named after the Australian pop star) at the Vicarage in 1989?

11. Where in the village did George Grundy persuade his mum Emma to go, against her wishes?

12. What work of art did Ruari buy for a less-than-delighted Jennifer?

GONE BUT NOT FORGOTTEN:
DORIS ARCHER

Born: 11 July 1890
Died: 26 October 1980
Played by: Gwen Berryman

Dan Archer's right-hand woman was the domestic crutch that supported Brookfield Farm for many years while her husband worked the farm. From her time as a lowly kitchen maid and lady's maid to Letty Lawson-Hope, Doris Archer saw nothing wrong with spending her days tending to the farmhouse and cooking up all kinds of homemade delights. As the years passed in Ambridge, Doris became attached to her daughter-in-law Peggy and growing flock of grandchildren, especially Shula. Family played an enormous part in the life of this devoted woman, and while she may have struggled with the arrival of Dan's opinionated sister-in-law Laura Archer she was dedicated to the happiness of her own brother, Tom Forrest, who went through the wringer when he was charged with manslaughter. Sociable and friendly, Doris played an active role in village activities and was a founding member of the Ambridge WI – she even represented them at a Buckingham Palace garden party. Her Christian faith helped her through tough times, but caused conflict when her daughter Christine wished to remarry in St Stephen's, something she felt was inappropriate. Old age brought with it blood-pressure problems, bad headaches and arthritis, but this delightful farmer's wife died peacefully in her chair at Glebe Cottage.

LISTENER PORTRAIT

When and why did you start listening? Since around the mid-1950s, with gaps.

What's your most memorable Ambridge moment? The incineration of Grace Archer.

Which character would you most like to meet? Brian Aldridge.

Which character drives you crazy? Goody Shula.

If you could make one change to *The Archers* it would be... to keep the same actors. If change is unavoidable, match voices as closely as possible.

John Blake, town planner

MEET THE CHARACTERS:
THE TUCKERS

When his beloved wife Betty died in 2005, Mike didn't think he would find love again. Then the dynamic Vicky burst into his life via ballroom dancing and they married in 2009. Four years later Vicky gave birth to Bethany, her much longed-for daughter. Bethany has Down's Syndrome, and when she was two-and-a-half the family moved to Birmingham to give her more opportunities. Before that, they lived next door to Mike's son Roy and his family. But only Roy lives there now. His calm home and working life with his wife Hayley was shattered when he had a brief affair with his – and Hayley's – boss at Lower Loxley, Elizabeth Pargetter. Hayley left Roy and took their daughter Abbie to stay with her mother in Birmingham. Roy was trying to mend bridges with daughter Phoebe when Hayley asked for a divorce.

Mike and Betty's daughter, Brenda, was engaged to Tom Archer, but broke it off in 2013. She had crazy adventures in Russia (which were documented *The Archers*' occasional sister show, *Ambridge Extra*), then moved to London and is now engaged to an as-yet-unheard chap named Adrian.

Mike, always an early riser, was happy for a number of years as Ambridge's milkman, working for the Grange Farm dairy. But the milk business has been under great pressure lately, and Mike made the difficult decision to sell up.

DID YOU KNOW?

❋ Mike lost the sight in one eye when he got hit by a hydraulic pipe, and he now wears an eyepatch.

- Betty Tucker came off the contraceptive pill without telling husband Mike before falling pregnant with Roy.

- Betty shared her birthday with the Queen Mother.

- Mike Tucker declared himself bankrupt in 1986, a low point in his life.

- Ballroom dancing has always been a big part of Mike's life. He and Betty used to tread the boards in village performances and he met his second wife Vicky at a dance class.

- Brenda Tucker once worked as a trainee journalist on Radio Borsetshire.

- Brenda's had some ill-advised entanglements, notably with Lilian's former toy boy Scott, and then with Lilian's self-centred son James. Perhaps unsurprisingly, Lilian and Brenda have never had a very close friendship, despite working together for a number of years.

- As a teenager, Roy Tucker was part of a racist gang that targeted Usha Franks (then Gupta). Hayley Tucker used to go out with John Archer before she got together with Roy – she and John met at the Ice House, a club in Birmingham.

- Hayley and Roy shared their first kiss on Millennium Eve on the village green. After a struggle to conceive, they were delighted to welcome baby Abbie into the family in 2008.

- Phoebe was the result of a youthful fling that Roy had with Kate Archer. When Kate swanned off to South Africa, Hayley and Roy made a home for her with them.

- Phoebe has always found Hayley to be more of a mother to her than Kate. However, she now lives with Kate (and Brian and Jennifer) at Home Farm.

WELCOME TO AMBRIDGE:
BROOKFIELD BUNGALOW

- This bungalow was originally built as a home for newly-weds Ruth and David Archer, who moved in on 12 September 1990.

- The home, situated in Little Field on Brookfield Farm, enjoys views of the river and has a garden.

- Ruth, David and family temporarily swapped homes with Phil and Jill Archer in 1999 when Jill injured her knee and found the bungalow's layout more suited to her recovery.

- Once Phil and Jill had moved permanently to Glebe Cottage, David and Ruth moved back into the main farmhouse. The bungalow provided an extra source of income as a holiday let, and then a home for Bert and Freda Fry. It was badly damaged in the floods of 2015.

• QUIZ NIGHT AT THE BULL •

FURRY, FOUR-LEGGED FRIENDS

1. What kind of animals did Lynda Snell bring to the church on Palm Sunday in 2003?

2. Who came up with the money-spinning fête attraction of performing seals Mutt and Jeff?

3. Whose horse is called Spearmint?

4. Which of the following animals is not a dog: Biff, Mitch, Tolly or Fly?

5. A peacock has been living at The Bull since 1993, but what is its name?

6. Who was known as 'the dog woman'?

7. Who tried to save Christine's horse Midnight from a stable fire, causing her own death in the attempt?

8. Ralph Bellamy commissioned a portrait of Lilian sitting on his horse – what was the horse's name?

9. Name the dog who tucked into Susan and Neil Carter's wedding cake in 1984.

10. Where are Majorie Antrobus's dogs Portia and Bettina buried?

11. What was the name of Will's dog which was shot by Ed?

12. Who has owned cats called Sammy, Bill and Ben?

MEET THE CHARACTERS: THE PERKS

Kathy married Sid Perks in 1987 and son Jamie came along in 1995. She was Sid's second wife, after Polly – but not his last. Sid and Kathy split up after his steamy affair with Jolene Rogers in 2000, whom he later married. Despite their divorce, Kathy was devastated when Sid died in 2010 in New Zealand, while visiting his daughter Lucy. Jolene has since married Kenton and moved on, but Kathy (who also had a long relationship with Kenton – she and Jolene clearly have the same taste in men) has not found lasting love. She has struggled at times with bringing up Jamie, particularly when he went through a tricky phase after she and Kenton separated. But Jamie got his act together at last and trained as a tree surgeon, a role to which he is greatly suited.

DID YOU KNOW?

❋ Sid was a nineteen-year-old Brummie with a criminal record when he arrived in Ambridge in 1963. Jack Woolley took a shine to the boy from his homeland and gave him a job as his chauffeur and handyman for four years.

❋ Sid took pretty Bull barmaid Polly Mead out on a date in 1964 to the Hollerton Fair, where his motorbike was stolen by thugs who knew him from his criminal past.

❋ As a child Lucy Perks wasn't allowed a puppy, so she imagined one called Crackers.

❋ Lucy went to Nottingham University to study ecological

science, but never graduated because she was distracted by future husband Duncan Gemmell.

- For her wedding to Sid, Kathy wore a silk dress and a string of pearls she borrowed from Peggy.
- Jamie Perks was conceived after his parents had taken a moonlit stroll on the beach in New Zealand.
- Sid met Jolene Rogers at the gym in Borchester – it was Eddie Grundy who revealed their affair to Kathy in front of a full house at The Bull.
- After her divorce from Sid, Kathy had a date with a man called Richard, who collected menus and was an expert on staplers.
- When Kathy and Kenton split up, Jamie Perks damaged the new bird hide at Arkwright Lake during a drunken gathering of his friends in his frustration.

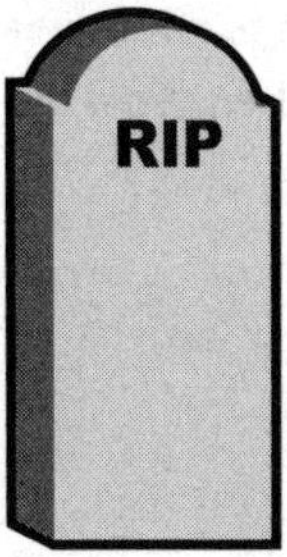

GONE BUT NOT FORGOTTEN: NIGEL PARGETTER

Born: 8 June 1959
Died: 2 January 2011
Played by: Graham Seed

Nigel Pargetter died after falling off the roof of his beloved family home, Lower Loxley Hall. At only 51 years old his departure was felt by many, but especially by his wife Elizabeth and their 11-year-old twins Lily and Freddie. Considered by some to have been born with a silver spoon in his mouth, the Rugby School-educated

Nigel did not always had it as easy as other Ambridge residents may have thought. His carefree youth saw him enjoying life but unsuited to hard work – he tried being a swimming pool salesman, working on a beef and maize farm in Zimbabwe and even dabbling in the stock exchange during the 1980s. But it was the death of his father, and the subsequent responsibility of the Lower Loxley Hall estate landing on his shoulders, that saw him finally grow up and take life a little more seriously.

The same could be said of his love life – an early interest in Shula Archer didn't amount to much, and he soon turned his attentions to her younger sister Elizabeth, whom he proposed to, although their immaturity saw the engagement broken and they went their separate ways. In 1992 Nigel hired Elizabeth to help him launch Lower Loxley Corporate Entertainments and together they began turning the decaying building and vast grounds into a profitable commercial enterprise. Brought closer by their work, they married in 1994 and had their children in 1999. Nigel's mother Julia may not have approved of common folk using the family home for 'green weddings' and other events, but it's certainly turned the fortunes of the stately home around. It's heartbreaking that Nigel is no longer around to see the fruits of his labour thrive, or his children grow up.

LISTENER PORTRAIT

When and why did you start listening? As a primary school-aged child I remember my mum listening, so it's always been in my mind. I can't remember exactly when I started listening regularly but it was probably around my late twenties.

What's your most memorable Ambridge moment? Why this I don't know, but Mark's funeral. I cried! And the whole Richard, Usha and Shula affair (but perhaps it's because Richard's back in town that I'm remembering it?).

Which character would you most like to meet? None of them!

Which character drives you crazy? Most of all, Helen. It was also Brenda. So so so glad she's gone... Shula close behind! Oh and Christine...

The Archers **is wonderful because...** it's escapism. Most of the time it's entertaining, and I can chat about it to my fellow *Archers*-listening friends. I kinda hate it to the point of liking it (weird, I know). When I feel crap and listen to it I realise all in my life is well really!

If you could make one change to *The Archers* **it would be...** I would make it less soap-opera-y. Maybe get the public to suggest storylines so it's a bit more real.

Anne Lavender-Jones, costumier

WELCOME TO AMBRIDGE: BROOKFIELD FARM

- This 469-acre mixed farm has grown, shrunk and grown again over the years.
- Brookfield used to be part of a three-farm cooperative before it incorporated the holdings of Marney's and Hollowtree by the end of the 1960s.
- Brookfield was struck twice by TB in the 1990s, and there was a scare in 2003 when the disease was found in a nearby farm.
- In 2001 David and Ruth Archer took over Brookfield when Phil retired and made the decision to contract out the arable farming to Home Farm.
- Despite bidding farewell to the pigs, the farm still boasts a 325-strong lambing flock. Brookfield lamb is marketed cooperatively under the Hassett Hills brand.
- The news of a possible road being built right through the farm – the infamous 'Route B' – led David and Ruth to make the difficult decision to sell up in 2014. Plans to move to Prudhoe in

Northumberland were very far advanced when David had a change of heart. After a certain amount of angst, the Archers renewed their plans to fight against the proposed route, as well as making contingency plans for continuing to farm, should the road get the go-ahead.

MEET THE CHARACTERS: THE ARCHERS OF THE BULL

It's fair to say that Kenton and Jolene had both been around the block before they got together in 2011. However, they were clearly right for each other and married two years later, with Jolene's daughter Fallon taking the role of best woman. Kathy Perks took news of Kenton's new relationship much better than might have been expected; after all, not only had Kathy and Kenton been a couple, but Jolene previously enticed Kathy's husband Sid away, too.

Kenton settled easily into the role he was born to play – pub landlord – and he and Jolene both worked hard to keep The Bull lively and profitable. Kenton was very supportive of Fallon, offering her funding for her tea shop with his expected share of the money from the sale of Brookfield. It was a massive blow to Kenton when this legacy failed to materialise, following

David's change of heart in February 2015. He discovered this at around the same time The Bull suffered flood damage, and just after Kenton and Jolene had taken a no-expense-spared trip to Australia. Kenton was furious with David, and found it hard to forgive him, or even be in the same room as him.

Jolene occasionally reflects on the career she might have had, as a country singer. She formed a new version of her old band, The Midnight Walkers, and they sang at Loxfest music festival, which put a spring in her step.

DID YOU KNOW?

- ✵ In 1982 Kenton Archer held the rank of Second Officer in the Merchant Navy.

- ✵ Jolene's real name is Doreen.

- ✵ Mel Archer, Kenton's first wife, called from Australia to tell in-laws Phil and Jill that she had married their son.

- ✵ In the 1980s, Jolene and Eddie formed a group called Big Eddie and the Lily of Layton Cross.

- ✵ Kenton bought an antiques shop from Nelson Gabriel (and promptly ran it into the ground).

- ✵ In 2003 he became the manager of Jaxx Caff in Borchester, which was owned at the time by Jack Woolley. Kenton later converted it to a trendy bar, simply called Jaxx.

- ✵ Kenton insisted that he take Jolene's stage costumes out of her wardrobe to make more room. He put them in the pub cellar, which flooded shortly afterwards (because he hadn't inspected the drains, despite Jolene asking him to). The costumes were ruined, and Jolene was not best pleased.

FARMING FESTIVITIES

Rural life is not all mucking out and mucking in – there's plenty of festive fun to be had too. Make sure you're not missing out on any of the social highlights in the Ambridge calendar by keeping track of these key annual events.

APPLE DAY

- Takes place every October, on or near the 21st and is usually held at Lower Loxley, on the village green or at one of the farms.

- Events and games have included bobbing for apples, apple and spoon races and seeing who can make the longest piece of apple peel.

- Apple identification competitions were held in 2001 (where a Pink Lady® tripped up Lynda Snell) and 2005 when tree warden George Barford was stumped by a sneakily placed Borsetshire Beauty.

- In 2012 Joe Grundy insisted on demonstrating his cider press without wearing his teeth, because they were hurting him. They later disappeared, to the consternation of all who had drunk some of his cider.

VILLAGE FÊTE

- This summertime event takes place between June and August, and has attracted a number of celebrity guests over the years.
- While some Ambridge fêtes focus on the more traditional delights of homemade produce stalls and the inevitable beer tent, other years feature many more unusual stalls and sideshows and even Miss Ambridge beauty queen competitions. Other past attractions include: a fortune teller (1980), Beautiful Baby competitions won by William Grundy in 1983 and Christopher Carter and Kylie Richards in 1990, a performance by the Edgeley Morris Dancers (1992), Bushtucker Trials (2004), Vegetable Olympics (2006), a town crier competition (2007), a caterpillar race with competitors wriggling along the ground inside sleeping bags (2012), Guess the weight of the calf (1979), yourself (1976) and the llama (2003), and even Pet Karaoke (1997). In 2013 the fête took the theme of the Highland Games, with tossing the fencepost a highlight, and Jazzer's bagpiping a lowlight.
- Walter Gabriel was an avid supporter of the fête throughout the 1960s and introduced a number of his own attractions to the proceedings, such as elephants Rosie and Tiny Tim, a hot-air balloon, a steam engine and even performing seals.
- In 1975 the first prize for the fête's talent competition (donated by Charles Harvey) was a £10 record token.

QUIZ NIGHT AT THE BULL

LEAVE IT UP TO FÊTE

1. Who did Phil Archer spot and film at the village fête in 1957?

2. What did Walter Gabriel name his village fête ventriloquist's dummy?

3. What year did the village fête host its own Bushtucker Trials?

4. What wartime-themed team name did Kathy Perks and Hayley Tucker give themselves in the fête in 2005?

5. When Susan Horrobin won a pig at the village fête in 1983, who offered to build a pen for it and would later became her boyfriend and husband?

6. Which well-known star of *The Dam Busters* cut the ribbon at the village fête in 1962?

7. In 1965 a hypnotist at the village fête managed to convince farm worker Ned Larkin a glass of water he was drinking was filled with what?

8. At the fête in 2014, Lynda tried, but failed, to catch Lilian out over her demonstration of which handicraft?

9. Who was described as 'the oldest torch bearer' at the 2012 fête's community games?

10. Which local author opened the 2011 fête, much to Jennifer's discomfort?

11. Which three men performed as an Andrews Sisters tribute band at the 2005 fête?

12. What were tossed instead of cabers at the 2013 fête's Highland Games?

WELCOME TO AMBRIDGE: GLEBE COTTAGE

✂ Set in a walled garden near to St Stephen's Church, this picturesque cottage has been in the Archer family for years.

✂ The small two-bedroom property was left to Doris Archer for her lifetime by her employer Letty Lawson-Hope for whom she worked as a kitchen maid and lady's maid.

✂ The house was rented out to a number of Ambridge folk until Doris and Dan bought the freehold and retired there. Their son Phil and his wife Jill would also retire there in 2001.

✂ When Phil and Jill's daughter Shula lived in the cottage, her husband Mark took on the hard task of rethatching the roof.

✂ Following a burglary in 2014, Jill became nervous living alone, and David and Ruth asked her to move in with them. Glebe Cottage lay empty till Carol Tregorran moved back to Ambridge and rented it from Jill. With Bert's help, Carol has been busy enhancing the garden.

MEET THE CHARACTERS: THE CARTERS

Neil and Susan Carter live in Susan's dream home, Ambridge View, which Neil built. Daughter Emma and her fiancé Ed Grundy moved in with Neil and Susan when finances were tight, but later started renting Ed's brother Will's house, No. 1 The Green. (Will and his family live at Greenwood Cottage, a property that came with Will's job as gamekeeper for Home Farm.) It was here, while watching the village Christmas lights go on, that Emma proposed marriage and Ed accepted. Emma's previous marriage to Ed's brother Will was one of the shorter unions in Ambridge's history: they were together for eleven months before she told him she'd rather be with Ed. There was some confusion as to the paternity of George, Emma's son, but he turned out to be Will's. Emma and Ed have gone on to have daughter Keira. Emma works as Ruth and David's much-needed cleaner at Brookfield. She is also a keen upcycler and baker.

Neil is a pigman through and through, though he has several other interests, including bell-ringing and cricket. He is also a churchwarden. Susan runs the community shop and is well-known as a source of vital village information, although she's on the record as saying that she doesn't like to gossip! Neil and Susan's son, Christopher, a farrier, is married to Alice Aldridge, Brian and Jennifer's daughter.

DID YOU KNOW?

- Neil failed his tractor proficiency test when he first started working as an apprentice at Brookfield Farm.

- Susan Carter (née Horrobin) is the oldest of six children. She has four brothers and a sister.

- Emma Carter was teased at school when her uncle Clive was involved in the village post office raid.

- Susan was sentenced to six months in prison in 1993 for harbouring a fugitive – her brother Clive.

- When he was nine, Christopher Carter trained his hamster to go round its wheel to music for the village fête.

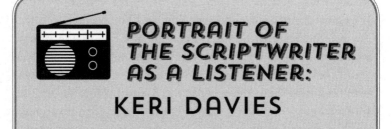

PORTRAIT OF THE SCRIPTWRITER AS A LISTENER:
KERI DAVIES

Keri Davies became a producer on The Archers *in 1992, and started writing scripts for it in 2003.*

When and why did you start listening? As a kid, I was exclusively a BBC Radio 1 listener. But when I applied to join the RAF (I was an officer for six years), I started listening to Radio 4 to brush up my current affairs knowledge. And if you listen to Radio 4, it's pretty impossible to miss *The Archers*. It was at the time of fun shenanigans with young Shula and Nigel, Mr Snowy, the gorilla suit and Nelson's wine bar. I was hooked for life.

What's your most memorable Ambridge moment? So many! But to pick one from the days when I was an *Archers* producer: Clive Horrobin's raid on the village shop in 1993. The writer was Sally Wainwright, who went on to write *Last Tango in Halifax*, among many other great dramas. It was a fabulous chance for me to flex my directing muscles early in my career.

The Archers is wonderful because... it gives work to the otherwise unemployable (me).

If you could make one change to *The Archers* it would be... a repeat of the Friday episode on Saturdays.

ISSUES IN AMBRIDGE:
AGRICULTURAL DISEASES

While agricultural storylines don't always take centre stage on *The Archers*, outbreaks of diseases such as foot-and-mouth and TB have sometimes had catastrophic impacts on the farms and characters on the show, with storylines running for months and in some cases over a year. Cases of foot-and-mouth disease occurred on UK farms throughout the twentieth century, and a number of cases were reported in the 1950s, before the major outbreak of 1967. One such case found its way to Brookfield Farm in 1956, when two pigs were reported sick by farmhand Simon. Dan Archer, suspecting the worst, called in the vet who tested the animals. They had the disease and Brookfield was quickly quarantined and PC

Bryden stood guard at the gate making sure no one came and went from the farm. As poignant and harrowing as it was listening to Dan and Doris remain on their farm while all their cloven-hoofed beasts were slaughtered, the story was also informative, explaining to the listeners about the possible cause of the outbreak, compensation from the Ministry and the importance of insuring against loss of income. The ten-month story saw Doris Archer considering giving up on farming altogether and the struggles the family faced while they built the farm back up after the cull.

The *Archers* writers made a number of last-minute changes to scripts at the start of 2001 when the largest outbreak of foot-and-mouth disease spread across the UK resulting in 2,000 cases of the disease and over 10 million sheep and cattle being slaughtered. While none of the Ambridge farms reported cases, the disease found its way to Little Croxley on the other side of Borchester and the effects were felt in Ambridge, with issues of disinfection, isolation and tourism being discussed.

Bovine tuberculosis has caused significant problems for Brookfield Farm. It first reared its head in 1994, when Phil was running the farm, in a storyline that lasted eighteen months. The slow-burning plot accurately illustrated the testing procedures and protocols carried out by vets and officials, the prolonged worry experienced by farmers while they wait for the verdict on their livestock, and the stigma attached to a farm after a positive diagnosis. The disease was brought to Brookfield again in 1994 and 1998, and a scare occurred in 2003 after there was a TB outbreak at nearby Bank Farm. More recently, David and Ruth battled an outbreak of Johne's disease in the Brookfield cattle in early 2011, which led to some of the animals being slaughtered. In 2014 their sheep suffered from sheep scab, which luckily is treatable if caught early enough. The same year, Shula's stables suffered from an outbreak of 'strangles', a bacterial infection which takes its name from the fact that it can cause the animal to have difficulty with swallowing food and even breathing.

In 2013 Ed Grundy's cows were afflicted with Neospora, an infection which causes cows to miscarry. This can be carried and spread by dogs, which might explain, though not excuse, the anger that led Ed to accidentally shoot his brother Will's dog.

WELCOME TO AMBRIDGE: GLEBELANDS AND THE GREEN

- ✂ This small development of executive homes near to the village green caused quite the Ambridge controversy when landowner Jack Woolley proposed building them in the 1970s.

- ✂ Laura Archer and Colonel Danby especially made sure the builders stuck rigidly to the plans when they were finally built in 1978 and 1979.

- ✂ Residents include Derek and Pat Fletcher and Mr and Mrs Patterson.

> ❦ The Green development opposite the village green was once home to Neil and Susan Carter, though they now live in their self-built house, Ambridge View. Their old place, No. 1 The Green, is currently owned by Will Grundy, and rented by Ed and Emma Grundy and their children. Meanwhile, the Horrobin family have been the long-time disreputable residents at No. 6 The Green.

GONE BUT NOT FORGOTTEN:
JOHN 'JACK' ARCHER

Born: 17 December 1922
Died: 12 January 1972
Played by: Denis Folwell

No parents should have to bury their children, so it was truly a sad day for Dan and Doris when Jack Archer died aged just 49 years old from liver failure. Their eldest son had lived a somewhat troubled life, despite his marriage to the gregarious Peggy and the birth of their three children (Jennifer, Lilian and Tony). He never quite achieved his full potential or truly believed in himself. The farmer's life is a hard one, full of uncompromising choices and physical work, which Jack quickly learned wasn't for him when he had his own Ambridge smallholding. A farming venture in Cornwall also proved unsuccessful when his partner became a little too fond of Peggy, so it was back to Ambridge for the family. The couple soon found themselves behind the bar at The Bull, in 1953.

While Peggy flourished as a natural landlady, Jack felt overshadowed and turned to the drink that was so readily available. A stint in hospital to deal with a nervous breakdown seemed to have helped Jack turn over a new leaf and he was keenly involved with his children – their schooling, their love lives (especially Jennifer's) and their dramas – most memorably when Jennifer found herself pregnant and refused to name the father. While much of his later life was spent using good business sense to buy and renovate the pub thanks to generous donations from his Aunt Laura, Jack couldn't shake off his demons and added gambling to his list of vices. Despite trying to give up drinking, the damage had been done and Jack found himself consigned to a clinic in Scotland battling liver disease. He missed his children's weddings, the births of grandchildren, and being there for wife Peggy through it all.

AND THE AWARD GOES TO...

�֍ Scriptwriter and actor Norman Painting (Phil) was awarded the OBE in the New Year's Honours list of 1976. That same year Gwen Berryman (Doris) was voted Midlander of the Year. She went on to receive an MBE at Buckingham Palace in 1981, a year after her character had died.

✖ The programme was awarded the prestigious Sony Radio Gold Award in May 1987.

✖ Patricia Greene (Jill) was awarded the MBE in 1997.

- June Spencer, who plays Peggy Woolley, was made an OBE in 1991. And in 2014 she was awarded a Lifetime Achievement prize at the BBC Audio Drama awards.

- In 2001, *The Archers*' fiftieth year, Trevor Harrison (Eddie Grundy) was awarded an MBE for his services to radio drama.

- At the Variety Club Showbusiness Awards in 2002, Felicity Finch (Ruth Archer) and Tim Bentinck (David Archer) accepted the Radio Personality Award on behalf of the programme.

- In 2003, Charles Collingwood, whose character Brian was the nation's most infamous philanderer at the time, was presented with the famous red book on television's *This Is Your Life*.

- In 2007, *The Archers* won a Mental Health Media award for its subtle and realistic portrayal of Jack Woolley's Alzheimer's disease.

- Graham Seed, who joined the programme as Nigel Pargetter in 1983 and whose character died in the dramatic sixtieth anniversary episode, was awarded Radio Broadcaster of the Year at the 37th Annual Broadcasting Press Guild Awards in 2011.

- In the same year, Ryan Kelly (Jazzer) won an Ability Media International award for broadcasting excellence and diversity.

- After 22 years at the helm of The Archers, former editor Vanessa Whitburn was made an OBE in 2013, in recognition of her services to radio drama.

QUIZ NIGHT AT THE BULL

HERE COMES THE BRIDE!

1. Which lady wore an apricot-coloured hat to her wedding in 1991?

2. Who was best man at the wedding of his ex-wife?

3. Whose was the first wedding to be heard on the air in 1955?

4. Who gave Polly Mead away at her wedding to Sid Perks because her own father was locked up in the county psychiatric hospital?

5. Who received a second-hand 1952 motor car as a wedding present from his new in-laws?

6. Mrs Ainsley of Churcham made a cream and gold dress for which bride in 1979?

7. Who accompanied Jennifer and Roger Travers-Macy on their post-wedding holiday to Ibiza?

8. Where did Lilian and Ralph Bellamy have their wedding reception?

9. In 1963 Janet Sheldon died four months after marrying which long-time bachelor?

10. Elizabeth Archer and Kate Aldridge were bridesmaids for which couple's nuptials in 1985?

11. Who spent her hen night sewing bunting?

12. Who lent Nic Hanson a garter for her 'something borrowed' when she married Will?

MEMORABLE MOMENTS:
ED BEING SICK ON SUSAN'S SOFA

Date: 24 October 2014
Location: Ambridge View

You have to feel sorry for Susan. Sometimes. When Ed and Emma lived at Ambridge View, Ed was forever tramping muddy boots into the house, or leaving his dirty dishes all over the kitchen. Then, one memorable evening, after several days of feeling sorry for himself over his financial woes and lack of luck (yes, we do realise that this doesn't really pin it down to one particular time), he got roaring drunk with Jazzer and Roy. Roy had his own troubles, and ended the night by going round to Lower Loxley and calling for Elizabeth outside her window. Meanwhile, Ed staggered home, bumped into Susan and drunkenly asked her for a hug, then was promptly sick all over her sofa. Listeners expressed themselves freely on Twitter. 'Well... that was a jarringly realistic barfing scene,' said @isaacq, while Susan got short shrift from @ChristchurchPom: 'Good old Ed. Susan's been asking for that for a long time.' And @ifwehadanyham imagined the scene the next day: '"12 cases of Febreze please". Susan phones the village shop's wholesaler.'

LISTENER PORTRAIT

When and why did you start listening? I got hooked staying with relations who had a market garden and told me how great it was – 1951.

What's your most memorable Ambridge moment? Dear Nigel slipping off the roof to his death.

Which character would you most like to meet? Brian Aldridge.

Which character drives you crazy? Susan Carter.

The Archers **is wonderful because...** however ungripping or annoying it can be, it just gets into another storyline and one goes on listening.

If you could make one change to *The Archers* **it would be...** As I'm fairly deaf, I'd like the characters to use each other's names much more during their conversations.

Bay Heriz Smith, potter

WELCOME TO AMBRIDGE: GRANGE FARM

- The Grundys used to be tenants here, but they were never afflicted too badly with a work ethic, and this – combined with a run of bad luck – forced them out of the farm due to bankruptcy in 2000.
- When Oliver Sterling first bought 50 acres of Grange Farm he stocked it with beef cattle, before having a change of heart, selling the herd off and replacing them with Guernseys to produce milk.
- When TB struck Oliver's herd in 2008 and he almost gave up farming altogether, Ed Grundy offered his services and took over as a tenant farmer. In 2012, Oliver and Ed decided to vaccinate the badgers on the farm, to try and prevent the spread of TB.
- The Guernsey milk from Grange Farm was used to make a semi-hard cheese called Sterling Gold, thanks to some help from Helen Archer. But in 2015 Ed decided he would have to sell the cows. He was already struggling financially with the business, but when Mike gave up his milk delivery, Ed knew it would be very difficult to find another local outlet.

MEET THE CHARACTERS: ROB TITCHENER

Brought in to manage the new mega-dairy Berrow Farm, Rob initially caused a few female hearts to flutter. He was cagey about why his wife Jess was still living in Hampshire, and soon Helen was hoping that Jess would stay there for good. She and Rob fell for each other, but Rob briefly gave his marriage a second go when Jess finally joined him in Ambridge. It was at a Christmas party, the first the new couple hosted, that their marriage fell apart, crashing as spectacularly as the whole salmon which got dropped. Jess fled, and Rob moved in with Helen and Henry.

One minute nice, the next not, Rob is a hard man to understand. He likes to be in control, proposing that fiancée Helen wear more restrained clothes, and discouraging her from working in the shop. And he has a temper: Shula witnessed this first hand when Rob shoved a hunt saboteur, and then lied about it. But Helen adores Rob, standing up for him when her parents expressed their concerns, and supporting him when pregnant Jess insisted she was carrying his child (she wasn't, as it turned out).

DID YOU KNOW?

- Rob likes nothing better than a glass of wine and a snuggle on the sofa with Helen, after Henry's gone to bed.

- He's estranged from his parents, who once cancelled a visit to Ambridge at the last minute (though it wasn't clear whether Rob had definitely invited them).

- Ian Craig landed a punch on Rob after they crossed the finishing line at the 2014 Rough and Tumble Challenge, which was witnessed by special guest Sir Bradley Wiggins.
- It was thanks to Rob that Tom fled to Canada after jilting Kirsty – Rob used his connections to find Tom a job over there.

MAKING THE ARCHERS: FARMING FANS AND ARCHERS ADDICTS

In a time of HD 3D televisual experiences it's comforting to know that *The Archers* remains the world's longest-running drama series – an astounding achievement. With nearly five million listeners tuning in every week in the UK alone, the programme is going from strength to strength. *The Archers* is broadcast from Sunday to Friday at 7 p.m. each evening. Each episode is repeated the following day (except on Saturdays – there's no repeat of Friday's episode). If you miss the show during the week you can always catch up with the omnibus edition at 10 a.m. on Sundays, listen to episodes on the BBC iPlayer or download them from your favourite podcasting app.

The Archers' loyal listeners have helped to make it the most popular non-news programme on Radio 4 and the most listened-to programme online. The *Archers* production team and actors love to meet the listeners at festivals, book signings and the launch of Eddie Grundy's CDs. There have even been *Archers* conventions – in 1994 one was held in Malvern, Worcestershire, opened by *EastEnders* actress Wendy Richard. The show's official fan club, Archers Addicts, run by members of the cast, held events at Pebble Mill Studios, where the show used to be recorded, so fans could meet the cast and see how the show is put together. Still can't get enough of Ambridge? Past theatre tours of *The Ambridge Pageant* (1991) and *Murder at Ambridge Hall* (1993) saw members of the cast appear in live *Archers* productions, while on Boxing Day 2014 a radio performance of Lynda's production of *Blithe Spirit* was broadcast, with parts played by members of the cast. It was once possible to set sail on an *Archers* cruise with some of your favourite characters. Fred. Olsen Cruise Lines gave fans the chance to meet the cast, learn about how the programme's sound effects were made and watch a live 'recording' taking place.

Archers listeners are passionate and proactive, and some regularly contribute to a number of unofficial websites discussing characters, storylines and reminiscing over the last sixty-odd years of *Archers* history. Many have created spoof Twitter accounts for their favourite characters: Elizabeth, Eddie, Tom, Fallon and countless others all have a presence on Twitter. Even Bartleby, Joe Grundy's beloved pony, tweets. To find out more about these accounts, as well as *Archers*-related podcasts and more, have a look at *Archers* Extra on p.221.

• QUIZ NIGHT AT THE BULL •

DOCTOR, DOCTOR!

1. Phil Archer was on a business trip in which country when he was hospitalised with an infected foot?

2. In 1958 Pru Forrest spent six months in a sanatorium after being diagnosed with what?

3. Who was admitted to Felpersham Isolation Hospital with diphtheria in 1952?

4. Who did Carol Grey knock off their scooter when she arrived in the village in 1954?

5. Who fell through the ice of the village pond, only to be rescued by her father and Ned Larkin in 1958?

6. Which child was bitten by an adder in 1977?

7. What frozen dish did Freda Fry drop on her foot in 1995?

8. Who infected the entire cast of the 2008 pantomime with flu?

9. What bone did Nigel Pargetter break during his quad bike race with Kenton?

10. Shula was somewhat relieved when son Daniel was diagnosed with systemic juvenile rheumatoid arthritis because she thought he had what illness instead?

11. What was the name of the little girl who was hospitalised with the *E. coli* bug after eating Bridge Farm ice-cream?

12. Why was James Bellamy in hospital in 2012?

FACT FILE: FORMER CAST MEMBERS

- **Bob Arnold** was one of two actors who played Doris Archer's brother Tom Forrest, but after his first audition for the programme, Bob was told he would never be on the show due to his recognisable accent, since he had already worked on programmes such as *In the Cotswolds*, *Children's Hour* and other radio plays. Four months later, producers changed their mind and asked him to be part of the programme.
- **Ballard Berkeley** (Colonel Danby) may have played a colonel on *The Archers* and a major in *Fawlty Towers* but in reality he spent World War Two working for the Metropolitan Police.
- In his role as the Reverend Richard Adamson, **Richard Carrington** presided over the funeral of Doris Archer. This was recorded for the programme only a week after the death of the actor's own father.
- **Pamela Craig** may have played Mike Tucker's dutiful wife Betty on the programme for many years, but the actress also spent thirteen weeks on *Coronation Street* as Jackie Marsh, a journalist who had an affair with Ken Barlow.
- As Sid Perks, **Alan Devereux** got to keep an eye on his own daughter Tracy-Jane, who played Sid's daughter Lucy on the programme.
- **Norman Painting** played Phil Archer on the show for nearly 60 years, making him a Guinness World Record holder for the longest continuous performance in the same role. Painting also wrote about 1,200 episodes of the programme under the pseudonym Bruno Milna.

- Before **Graham Roberts** stepped into George Barford's boots he played tennis in the qualifying rounds at Wimbledon and rowed in the Henley Royal Regatta.

- **Colin Skipp** was nearly 30 when he auditioned (successfully) for the role of 16-year-old Tony Archer in 1967. When he retired from the role in 2014 on health grounds, he was at that time the longest-serving actor in a British soap opera. In a newspaper interview he compared himself to Tony, saying, 'while at 60 years of age, Tony quickly recovered from his heart attack, I had more problems at 74 coping with several real-life heart attacks'. He sent his best wishes to his successor in the role, David Troughton, and said that he hoped 'the part will give him as much pleasure as it gave me'.

- **Haydn Jones**, who played Joe Grundy, died on his way to the studio to record an episode of the show in 1984. He was replaced by Edward Kelsey, who for over 30 years has made the role indisputably his own and become a firm favourite with listeners.

WELCOME TO AMBRIDGE: GRANGE SPINNEY

- Dubbed the Wisteria Lane of Ambridge, these executive homes lie between the churchyard and Grange Farm.
- Grange Spinney residents Sabrina and Richard Thwaite have a large conservatory and a 4x4.
- There are twelve luxury homes and six low-cost homes in the development.
- Most residents commute to Birmingham for work and shop in Felpersham, not playing much part in the life of the village.
- Other residents living in Grange Spinney are the Noakeses and their daughter (who goes to boarding school), Barry Simmonds, Mrs Palmer, the Hendricks, the Robinsons, the McWilliamses and the Thompsons.
- Hilary Noakes and the Thwaites were among those who took refuge in St Stephen's when Grange Spinney was flooded.

LISTENER PORTRAIT

When and why did you start listening? I don't recall exactly, as it was always on in my house as I was growing up, so it is a real early childhood memory. My first word was 'tractor', which probably was influenced by Phil Archer.

What's your most memorable Ambridge moment? It is the sad events that stick in my mind... the deaths of John and Phil Archer are memorable moments.

Which character would you most like to meet? Without doubt, Joe Grundy. I would love to spend an evening in the pub with Joe (and Eddie) discussing the finer points of life. Ferrets, etc.

Which character drives you crazy? I have never been able to warm to Ruth Archer. She has driven me to distraction right from the early days when she started dating David.

The Archers **is wonderful because...** it is like a favourite cuddly blanket. You can snuggle in and forget your worries for ten minutes every evening... Well, apart from when Ruth is on.

If you could make one change to *The Archers* it would be... It has a habit of promoting one type of agriculture (the organic, fluffy side), whilst damning commercial farming. This gives an unbalanced impression of the agricultural sector to the wider public. I would like them to paint a better picture of larger-scale agriculture and the benefits it can bring. Not all large-scale farming is conducted in the style of Borchester Land!

Duncan Rawson,
Partner, European Food and Farming Partnerships

GONE BUT NOT FORGOTTEN:
MARJORIE ANTROBUS

Born: 1922
Died: 12 August 2008
Played by: Margot Boyd

Married life for Marjorie Antrobus was truly a joy as she travelled the world with husband Teddy on his various army postings. After his death in Nairobi, Marjorie returned to the UK and settled in Borsetshire's Waterley Cross, where she bred Afghan hounds – her other true joy in life. One of her hounds even picked up second prize at Crufts. She fell in love with Ambridge after she visited to speak at the Over Sixties Club and moved into Nightingale Farm shortly after. As an Ambridge resident Marjorie got stuck into village life as a bell ringer, acted and sung in village performances, and became an invaluable cricket scorer. She was always closely associated with St Stephen's and supportive of its various vicars, and while she never fell in love again she made some true friends, especially in her lodger Hayley Jordan (now Tucker) who helped her when she developed problems with her sight. After many years of village life, not to mention that surprising blind date with a 'Gentleman farmer seeking companionship' aka Joe Grundy, Marjorie moved into The Laurels retirement home where she passed away.

QUIZ NIGHT AT THE BULL

LONG ARM OF THE LAW

1. How many years was Clive Horrobin sentenced to, for the arson attack which destroyed George and Christine Barford's home?

2. What crime was Matt Crawford imprisoned for, in 2009?

3. Whose imprisonment in 1993 led to the campaign known as 'Free the Ambridge One'?

4. Who discovered that his illegitimate daughter, Rosemary Tarrant, was a policewoman?

5. Who had to face police questioning after overdosing on ketamine?

6. Why did PC Harrison Burns arrest Fallon's father Wayne Tucson at Loxfest?

7. What did Shula tell the police, when questioned about the fight she witnessed between Rob and a hunt saboteur?

8. Why did Tom and Kirsty face criminal charges in 1999?

9. Before becoming a gamekeeper, what was George Barford's profession?

10. Who had an affair with PC Dave Barry?

11. Who shopped Keith Horrobin to the police for setting fire to the barn at Brookfield?

12. What illegal activity did Darrell unwillingly become involved in organising?

MEET THE CHARACTERS: THE ALDRIDGES

Despite being amongst the wealthiest inhabitants of Ambridge, Brian and Jennifer have not always had the happiest of marriages. Brian's liking for the ladies has caused more than a few bumps in the road, and a bump elsewhere too, when he got lover Siobhan Hathaway pregnant. Their son, Ruairi Donovan, born in 2002, was the most controversial addition to the Aldridge clan. He was brought back to Ambridge from Ireland by Brian after Siobhan died of cancer in 2007. Ruairi currently spends most of his time at boarding school, but when he's at home, it's Jennifer who does most of the parenting. Jennifer was not a blushing bride when she married Brian, however. She already had two children, Adam and Debbie, by two other men. Brian and Jenny also have two children together, Kate and Alice.

Adam and Alice are settled, more or less, with their partners. Adam works for Home Farm, as does Debbie, though she lives in Hungary, and runs Home Farm's arable business by email. She was recently relieved of her other role, that of managing Berrow Farm for Borchester Land.

In 2001 Kate married journalist Lucas Madikane and they moved to his native South Africa, where they had two children, Noli and Sipho. In 2014 Kate returned to Ambridge, officially to study for (yet another) course in international development at Felpersham University. It was soon revealed, however, that Lucas had thrown her out after discovering that she'd been having an affair. Kate was desperate to reconnect with her daughter Phoebe, but her somewhat unfortunate manner only succeeded in driving them further apart. Phoebe, who attends Borchester

Green secondary school, lives at Home Farm with Kate, Brian and Jennifer since the separation of Roy and Hayley, her dad and stepmum.

DID YOU KNOW?

- Adam's father was Brookfield farmhand Paddy Redmond, and Adam's birth led to Jennifer becoming the first single mother in Ambridge, in 1967. Jennifer's unsuccessful first marriage was with Debbie's father, Roger Travers-Macy, who had previously dated her sister Lilian.
- Brian Aldridge's wandering eyes have fallen on the likes of Caroline Bone, riding instructor Mandy Beesborough, and even Betty Tucker (who was wise enough to turn down his skinny-dipping offer) during his marriage to Jennifer. But it was his affair with Siobhan Hathaway that Jennifer found hardest to forgive.
- Brian in turn objected to Jennifer's close relationship with the late John Tregorran.
- When he was a child, Adam was bitten by an adder while out riding with friends in Heydon Berrow – he was rushed to hospital and saved by a new anti-venom serum.
- Debbie finally ended her relationship with ex-husband and university lecturer Simon Gerrard after walking in on him sharing a passionate kiss with his department head's wife in 2001. For a while she had a boyfriend in Hungary called Marshall, and brought him home to meet Brian and Jenny, but they've now split.
- Phoebe Aldridge was born in a tepee at the Glastonbury Festival.

✂ Alice spent some of her gap year working on an AIDS project in Africa with her sister Kate. More recently, she travelled abroad again – this time to Las Vegas, where she married Chris Carter. Clearly her wanderlust was not satisfied, for she applied for – and got – a job in Canada. But after much soul-searching, she decided not to take it.

✂ In 2012, Adam had a fling with a Polish fruit-picker called Pavel, but luckily Ian never found out.

FAMOUS FACES IN AMBRIDGE: PART 2

Some more celebrities to grace the humble Ambridge folk with their presence…

★ **Terry Wogan** made an appearance on the show in 1989 when he popped into Grey Gables to participate in Jack Woolley's celebrity golfing weekend. Wogan's Radio 2 programme also raised £17,000 for Children in Need in 2005 by auctioning off a speaking part in *The Archers* – Wogan appeared as himself again alongside the winning bidder, Christine Hunt, who took on the previously unvoiced character of Grey Gables receptionist Trudy Porter. In the episode, Terry remembers Trudy participating in a quiz that he hosted.

★ **Judi Dench** breathed life (and a voice) into Pru Forrest when she appeared alongside Wogan for the show's 10,000th episode in 1989. The quiet character plucked up the courage to give the welcome speech when Terry arrived at Grey Gables for a celebrity golf tournament.

★ Although she didn't speak herself, **Esther Rantzen** joined Terry and Judi in the studio to record the sound effects, including the sound of a telephone being answered, which went along with their 1989 landmark episode.

★ Radio DJ **John Peel**, himself a life-long fan of *The Archers*, got to fulfil a dream of appearing on the show when in 1991 Radio 1 hosted their annual Christmas dinner at Grey Gables.

★ When Bond girl **Britt Ekland** took to the stage for Borchester's Christmas pantomime of *Aladdin* in 1992, Eddie Grundy persuaded his boys to enter a colouring competition to see the show and meet her backstage – and they won. On true Grundy form, Eddie got a little sloshed on champagne in Britt's dressing room. Some of this episode was recorded at the Birmingham Hippodrome.

★ And when Lynda Snell needed help getting the Village Hall refurbished in 1993, she called on fundraising challenge legend **Anneka Rice**, who arrived in the village ready to get stuck in.

WELCOME TO AMBRIDGE: GREY GABLES

- Ambridge's country house hotel is nestled in 15 acres of gardens.

- The four-star hotel was built in the Victorian era in a neo-Gothic style and houses 24 en-suite bedrooms. There is also an annexe with a further 36 bedrooms.

- The Royal Garden Suite is considered to be the best set of rooms in the hotel complex.

- In response to the recession chef Ian Craig started serving more affordable bistro fare in addition to the hotel's highly-reputed haute cuisine.

- Guests can enjoy a spot of golf at the nearby Ambridge Golf Club, a day of shooting on Home Farm, or an indulgent treat in the Health Club with its indoor pool, gym, sauna and jacuzzi.

- The hotel has mixed reviews on TripAdvisor, but there is much praise for the fine food and helpful staff. One reviewer praises the 'local Ambridge Organics flapjacks' in the room as a 'welcome alternative to the usual plastic packaged biscuits you get in chain hotels'. Another says of the local countryside: 'Great walks close by, but don't feed the llamas, you will get told off!' However, not everyone was impressed. One guest commented, 'I have to agree with other reviewers that standards here have sadly declined, which is a great shame, as I've been visiting Ambridge for most of my life.' And one visitor, who turned up shortly after the 2015 floods, wailed, 'I was expecting a night in a high-class establishment but instead was presented with a writhing mass of humanity, an old beggar dressed in a onesie and to cap it off, a ferret in my bed. I shall not be returning any time soon!'

- The Lodge guards the driveway to Grey Gables and is home to Peggy Woolley – she moved there in 1991 with late husband Jack.

- Grey Gables was a sanctuary during the 2015 floods, when it took in large numbers of refugees, including the Grundys and the Snells.

GONE BUT NOT FORGOTTEN:

PHILIP 'PHIL' ARCHER

Born: 23 April 1928
Death: 12 February 2010
Played by: Norman Painting

Taking the torch from his father Dan Archer, Phil became one of the most respected and trusted patriarchs in Ambridge. His long, loving relationship with wife Jill was a model marriage that lasted for 53 years. In the early days of *The Archers* it looked as if nothing could go wrong for young Phil, with his Farm Institute education, as he managed farms for the likes of George Fairbrother and Charles Grenville. The tragic loss of first wife, Grace, in a horrendous fire at Grey Gables could have broken him, but Phil found Jill shortly after, and started life afresh. He soon found himself incredibly busy with their four children – twins Shula and Kenton, followed by singletons David and Elizabeth. Brookfield Farm was Phil's responsibility when his father finally retired and became the focal point for many of the family's dramas – tensions between sons Kenton and David, Shula's disastrous relationships and Elizabeth's heart problems.

Later in life, Phil was reminded of the tragic loss of Grace by son-in-law Mark Hebden's death and daughter-in-law Ruth Archer's breast cancer. Through the highs and lows of Ambridge life Phil found joy in music – he played the organ at church and the piano for the Christmas plays – and his dear pigs. Brookfield was hard for Phil to leave, but a chance accident, which left Jill on crutches, found the couple trading places with David and Ruth and temporarily occupying the bungalow. They soon left the farmhouse for good and moved into Glebe Cottage, passing the family business to son David. Phil lived out his final years in the relative peace of Ambridge, finally able to devote time to his passion for astronomy, and to discovering the delight of baking, much to Jill's frequent frustration! In early 2010, he was found dead by Jill, sitting in his chair with Elgar's *The Dream of Gerontius* playing in the background.

PORTRAIT OF THE POET AS A LISTENER: WENDY COPE

Wendy Cope is an award-winning poet, whose collections include Making Cocoa for Kingsley Amis *and* Family Values. *She talks a little more about Ambridge in her collection of essays,* Life, Love and The Archers.

When and why did you start listening? At boarding school when I was about eight. The matron got us to vote on having a bedtime story or listening to *The Archers*. I voted for the story but *The Archers* won.

Which character would you most like to meet? Nigel was my favourite. Since they killed him off, I have been boycotting the programme. Haven't listened to it once. Don't miss it at all.

Which character drives you crazy? The one who used to annoy me most was Jennifer, with Shula and David as runners-up.

MEET THE CHARACTERS: CAROLINE AND OLIVER STERLING

Until she met Oliver, Caroline was not lucky in matters of the heart. She had one of the shorter Ambridge marriages when her soulmate, Guy Pemberton, died just seven months after their wedding. Before that, there was a broken engagement with vet/vicar Robin Stokes, and an ill-fated liaison with cad Cameron Fraser, not to mention an affair with Brian. However, when the handsome, cultured Oliver moved to the village following his divorce, the two fell in love. They married in 2006, and in the same year bought Grey Gables from Jack Woolley. Oliver took up gentleman-farmer-type activities including running a small beef herd, then a dairy business, and creating his own cheese, Sterling Gold, in partnership with Helen Archer. Oliver and Caroline trained as foster carers and looked after several young people, including Carly and Bruno. But Caroline's time became increasingly taken up with Grey Gables, particularly after her manager, Roy Tucker, left to work at Lower Loxley. Oliver began to feel that he never saw his wife, and urged her to get some more help.

DID YOU KNOW?

- Caroline's first job in Ambridge was as a barmaid at The Bull, working for Sid Perks.
- Oliver's middle name is Peregrine, while his ex-wife has the less fanciful name of Jane.
- Caroline is Will Grundy's godmother.
- Caroline has been on unsuccessful dates with Larry Lovell (Lynda's theatrical rival), and land agent Graham Ryder.

• QUIZ NIGHT AT THE BULL •

BULLSEYES, BALLS AND WICKETS

1. In what year did the cricket pitch move temporarily from the village green to Grey Gables?

2. Who was captain of The Bull's regular darts team in 1989?

3. Which two colours did the Ambridge Wanderers football team wear in 1975?

4. Who is the Single Wicket Competition played in memory of?

5. Four people have won the annual Single Wicket Competition twice. Who are they?

6. Whose cottage was the Ambridge Wanderers' pitch situated behind?

7. Who managed the Ambridge cricket team in 2009?

8. What sport is played to compete for the Viking Trophy?

9. Who was the cricket pavilion named after in 2007?

10. Women were allowed to the cricket club dinner for the first time in 1988 after a petition was organised by which female resident?

11. Who did Alistair bring in to run the youth coaching in 2010?

12. Only one woman has ever won the Single Wicket trophy – who?

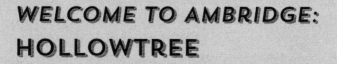

WELCOME TO AMBRIDGE: HOLLOWTREE

✂ This former farm, once known as Allard's Farm, was bought by Phil Archer in 1962 and was renamed by Phil, Jill and their family when they moved into the farmhouse.

✂ The house was converted into flats by Nelson Gabriel in the 1970s, but the 'farm' was later bought back by Phil to serve as a home for Brookfield's pigs.

✂ Phil was once heard playing a piano that had been abandoned by Joe and Eddie on the premises.

✂ Rex and Toby Fairbrother were just about ready to quit their geese-rearing plan for want of a piece of land. Then Pip strongly encouraged David to let them rent five acres and some buildings at Hollowtree. David reluctantly agreed, insisting this was on a temporary basis only, and the brothers assured him that was fine. That they then put up a tent on the land and branded their products as Hollowtree Geese should surely cause David no concerns...

MEET THE CHARACTERS:
THE HEBDENS
AND LLOYDS

Shula's first husband, Mark Hebden, was killed in a car crash in 1994. He never met his son Daniel, who was born later that year. When Daniel was young and unwell due to arthritis, Shula had an ill-advised affair with the doctor, Richard Locke, causing him to break up with Usha Gupta, his live-in partner. However, Shula later found stability with vet Alistair Lloyd, and they married in 1999. (Though her friendship with Usha was permanently damaged.)

Daniel, who prefers to be known as Dan, went into the army after leaving school, and has recently been made a second lieutenant. His surname is Hebden Lloyd, in acknowledgement of the fatherly role Alistair has played in his life.

When Jim Lloyd, Alistair's father, moved to Ambridge, it seemed his chief pleasure was to needle Shula. However, things settled down and Jim, a retired professor of history, found a new lease of life with his friends, his involvement in village life and his vintage car. His slightly surprising friendship with Jack 'Jazzer' McCreary led to the Glaswegian moving in as Jim's tenant, giving new meaning to the phrase 'The Odd Couple'.

DID YOU KNOW?

✂ Mark Hebden was once the Borchester Under-14 Judo Champion; later in life, he was kicked in the head by a deer he was trying to rescue from a lurcher.

✂ Joanna Hebden's mum put her on a diet when she was two stone overweight to try and help her slim down for her brother Mark's wedding to Shula.

✂ Mark proposed to Shula on Lakey Hill. They returned there after losing their first baby through an ectopic pregnancy and shouted into the wind.

✂ When Bunty Hebden gave daughter-in-law Shula some swan-patterned curtains, Shula said they looked like vultures and gave them to Clarrie Grundy.

✂ On the night Mark died, Shula Hebden was hosting Caroline Bone's hen party.

✂ Alistair went through a dark phase in 2008 when his gambling got out of control. He found support at Gamblers Anonymous and, under the surprising mentorship of gloomy butcher Maurice Horton, was able to recover. But he and Shula were forced to remortgage The Stables in order to pay off poker debts owed to Matt Crawford.

✂ Bunty and Reg, Mark's parents, both died in 2013, just a few months apart.

✂ Daniel weighed 7 lb 12 oz when he was born.

ISSUES IN AMBRIDGE:
COMMUNITY

Farming may take up a lot of people's time in Ambridge, but social and community issues cause just as much discussion, disagreement and drama. Contentious issues are often drawn from real problems or debates happening around the country, and in turn *The Archers*' portrayal of them can have a knock-on effect in other communities. A clear example of this is the storyline involving the community taking over Ambridge's village shop and running it with volunteers to prevent its closing. As village shops have seen a rise in closures over recent years, the programme's writers consulted with the Plunkett Foundation – an organisation that helps communities to set up and run a shop – when penning the scripts. With the Ambridge residents having a go at keeping their local amenities alive, and the Foundation being mentioned on the programme, there has been a steady rise in the number of community-run shops since its broadcast. And life imitates *The Archers* in other areas. For instance, before his untimely death in 2011, Nigel Pargetter had a wild idea for Lower Loxley to generate income, encourage environmentalism and yield local produce: allotments. By dedicating some of the estate's ancestral parkland into rentable allotment spaces, Nigel's plan inspired real-life Worcester farmers to turn one of their fields into an allotment space for growing fruit and vegetables.

After a few towns such as Totnes and Lewes introduced their own currency, Ambridge followed suit, and for a short while a 'TEA' (Transition Equivalents in Ambridge) was legal tender. It seemed to become unworkable fairly quickly, and has quietly been dropped.

In the past, characters have protested and campaigned for schools not to be closed, new housing not to be built and roads not to destroy their countryside. Most recently, the SAVE campaign has been vigorously campaigning against the proposed 'Route B' link road, which would go right through Bookfield, splitting the farm in two. This has generated a great deal of debate, with many people comparing the storyline to real-life road proposals in their own areas. The Campaign to Protect Rural England wrote about Route B in the context of calling a halt to what the government claims is the largest road-building programme for fifty years. The CPRE spokesman commented drily that, 'I suspect that the Mrs Penny Hasset who wrote to me asking CPRE to campaign against the road may not be a real person.'

FLOWER AND PRODUCE SHOW

Ambridge's gardeners take their green-fingered skills very seriously and each mid-September (although it was held in August in the mid-1980s) they have the opportunity to dazzle the opposition at this judged event in the Village Hall.

The top prizes at the Show are The Lawson-Hope Cup, The Valerie Woolley Memorial Cup and The Nelson Gabriel Memorial Cup for Gentleman's Buttonhole. The Show's overall winner is the competitor who receives the most first prize placements.

Some past overall winners include:

Jean Harvey:	1975, 1977 and 1979 (although she was disqualified in 1979 for using a professional gardener)
Pru Forrest:	1982, 1985 (with a record fifteen prizes), 1991
Freda Fry:	1990
Tom Forrest:	1993
Bert Fry:	1993, 2003

In some years the Flower and Produce Show has been replaced by other events, including a flower festival, a ploughing contest and a giant car boot sale.

The Show is not without its village scandal and disagreements. Here are just some from years past:

- In 1977 Laura Archer challenged her sister-in-law Doris's first-prize lemon curd win, claiming that it was a jar she had given Doris.
- Tom Forrest was quite put out in 1994 when young Will Grundy won the best onion category, judged by the French

mayor of twinned village Meyruelle – Tom claimed this 'butcher' didn't know what he was talking about.

- A burst pipe in the Village Hall caused a mass evacuation during the Show in 2007, which gave Derek Fletcher his chance to switch the name labels on the runner beans so Bert Fry wouldn't win the category. Luckily, Phil Archer switched them back and Bert took the title.
- Oliver won the Great Ambridge Bread Bake Off (men only) in 2012, while Jazzer was disqualified for using a bread maker.
- Walter Gabriel accused Pru Forrest of cheating her way to the overall prize winning position in 1982 by using products from the WI in the homemade jams category.
- Lynda Snell beat Tom Forrest to first prize in the marrow category in 1995, despite the fact he had given her the seed for her plant.
- Joe Grundy was the vegetable judge in 2010, and muddled up the entries, awarding Bert the prize for onions when he meant it to go to Jim.
- Pru Forrest neglected to feed husband Tom in her 1985 bid for overall winner – he became the subject of village gossip and snide jaunts from his friends at the pub.
- In 2008 Sabrina Thwaite swapped some jam jars for Jill's fruit cake, then entered Jill's cake into the competition and won first prize.
- In 2013 Helen won first prize in the craft competition, with a necklace she had bought. This was out of character for the usually scrupulously honest Helen, but it wasn't entirely her fault. She had invented a jewellery-making class as cover

for her clandestine meetings with her lover Rob, and when mum Pat pushed her into showing her something she'd made, Helen produced the necklace. Pat was so impressed by Helen's supposed jewellery talents that she entered the piece into the competition on her daughter's behalf, to Helen's complete embarrassment.

GONE BUT NOT FORGOTTEN:
FREDA FRY

Died: 13 March 2015

A very softly-spoken lady, popular Freda passed away after contracting pneumonia. Although she was one of Ambridge's most famous silent characters, her presence was felt throughout the community, and she is greatly missed. For many years the cook at The Bull, she was famous for her pies, while her cakes and jams usually did very well at the Flower and Produce Show. Though widely considered to be a bit of a homebody, she and husband Bert could be adventurous. They travelled to India for their golden wedding anniversary, and Freda briefly experimented with Indian cooking on their return. As well as Bert, Freda left behind a son (Trevor) and granddaughter (Amy). Not to mention dozens of pub customers who will never taste the likes of her hotpot again.

LISTENER PORTRAIT

When and why did you start listening? I started listening to Radio 4 towards the end of my thirties. Whenever *The Archers* theme tune came on, it took me straight back to my childhood. My mum has always listened every evening just before supper. In fact, the end of *The Archers* signalled supper time, and as a child who was permanently ravenous, it was a welcome sound. As an adult, at first, I began listening in an ironic/guilty-pleasure type way, but now I am well and truly hooked.

What's your most memorable Ambridge moment? Tom Archer jilting Kirsty. This was the storyline that first reeled me in. As a newbie, I didn't know Kirsty well as a character, but I have to say I found her extremely annoying and was glad Tom finally found the guts to call it off. Although, the way the village vilified him, you'd have thought he'd murdered someone.

Which character would you most like to meet? None of them, it would just ruin it.

Which character drives you crazy? Helen. Her inability to see how awful and controlling Rob is is utterly infuriating. Oh and Lilian's voice drives me bananas.

***The Archers* is wonderful because...** it is a comforting constant in life, ten minutes of daily escapism.

If you could make one change to *The Archers* it would be... fewer storylines like Jennifer's new kitchen and escaped ferrets.

Rosy Muers-Raby, medical student

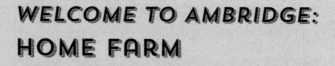

WELCOME TO AMBRIDGE: HOME FARM

- The sale of parts of the Bellamy Estate in the 1970s led to the creation of Home Farm.
- Home Farm has the largest farmhouse in Ambridge, with a solar-heated swimming pool and luxuriously decorated rooms. Jennifer's state-

of-the-art new kitchen took so long to be finished that Brian despaired of ever eating a home-cooked meal again. But now the Aldridges delight in their Umbrian tiles and boiling water tap. Jenny briefly alienated Pat, Clarrie and Susan by offering them her old kitchen cabinets, but Susan at least was mollified by being invited to Jennifer's party to celebrate the new room.

- Holiday cottage 'The Rookeries' used to be three farm workers' cottages.
- Brian Aldridge diversified the farm in the 1990s when he opened a riding course and a fishing lake on the land.
- The 1,585-acre farm is mainly arable with a small lambing flock and deer and is run by Adam Macy and his half-sister Debbie Aldridge.
- The farm's maze of maize has been designed in different years as a wizard (The Magi-maze), a spaceship (The Alien Maze) and a dinosaur (The Dino-maze).
- Home Farm's tied cottage has been home to Will Grundy since he returned from his honeymoon in Mexico with now ex-wife Emma. Back then, the cottage was called Casa Neuva ('new home' in Spanish). Will now shares this gamekeeper's cottage with new wife Nic. She suggested changing the name, and it's now known as Greenwood Cottage.

FAST FACTS ON FURRY FRIENDS

Animals play a huge part in Ambridge life – whether they're being raced, ridden, reared or rounding up the sheep, there's hardly a house in the village that's animal-free. From horses and hounds to llamas and peacocks, Ambridge has been home to a number of memorable creatures over the years.

DOGS

Baz   Will Grundy's dog, sadly shot dead by Ed
Bessie   John Archer's Labrador–Retriever cross
Bettina One of Majorie Antrobus's most colourful Afghans
Biff   Working sheepdog at Brookfield Farm
Butch   Walter Gabriel's bulldog was a gift from Debbie Glover; he was put down in 1972
Captain Jack Woolley's Staffordshire Bull Terrier was famed for eating Susan and Neil Carter's wedding cake
Fly   Working sheepdog at Home Farm
Hermes   Lynda Snell's Afghan puppy
Honey   Hazel Woolley's Bassett Hound was a tenth birthday present but was shot two years later for scaring a flock of sheep
Judy   Tom Forrest's spaniel died in 1961 and was replaced by a Labrador
Meg   Will Grundy's gun dog – died 2013 and was replaced briefly by Baz
Mitch   Formerly Greg Turner's gun dog, looked after by Will Grundy
Nell   Dan Archer's sheepdog
Portia   Another of Majorie Antrobus's dogs now buried in the garden at Nightingale Farm

Scruff	Daniel Hebden Lloyd's Alsatian cross, taken in by Lynda because he was too boisterous at The Stables. Missing, presumed drowned, in the floods
Timus	Phil Archer was given this corgi by Walter Gabriel and Bill Sawyer after his wife Grace's death
Trigger	Doris Archer's Jack Russell was born in 1964 and lived nearly twelve years
Trouncer	A replacement dog for Hazel Woolley's Honey
Turpin	Jack and Peggy's boxer

HORSES

Bartleby	Joe Grundy's pony
Basil	The original Palm Sunday donkey
Benjamin	This donkey, kept at The Stables, took over from Basil for Palm Sunday services
Christina	Paul Johnson's horse that ran at Scowell Bradon
Comet	Helen Archer's hairy, overweight pony, which had to be put down due to laminitis
Grey Silk	Jack Woolley once owned this race horse
Maisie	This horse was given to Caroline by Guy on her fortieth birthday in 1995
Midnight	Grace Archer was trying to save Midnight when she returned to the stable fire that took her life; Midnight was Christine Barford's horse
Monarch	Paul Johnson rode this beast at the Heybury Point-to-Point race in 1958
Mister Jones	Olympic showjumper Ann Moore spent part of 1974 training a young Shula Archer on her horse, Mister Jones, believing she had promise
Red Knight	Ralph Bellamy's horse that Lilian rode at the South Borsetshire Point-to-Point; Ralph commissioned a portrait of Lilian on Red Knight
Spearmint	Alice Carter's horse

| Tolly | Short for 'Autolycus', this Hanoverian cross thoroughbred was bought for Debbie by Brian Aldridge in 1992 |
| Tootsie | Otherwise known as Hassett Hill Two Timer, shared between Brian Aldridge (75%) and Christine Barford (25%) |

Other horses referred to at The Stables include: Marcie, Maxwell, Fleur, Minty, Colfax, Pluto, Sylvester, Nimrod, Silver, Cottonwood, Niobe, Magnet and Duff

OTHER ANIMALS

Daphne	Joe Grundy's ferret
Eccles	The proud peacock who moved into The Bull in 1993
Barbarella	Known by those that love her as 'Miss Babs', this Berkshire pig belongs to the Grundys
Bill and Ben	Joe Grundy gave these cats to Peggy after the death of her previous feline. Ben passed away just a few months after Jack Woolley died.
Constanza	One of Lynda's llama birthday presents to husband Robert
Demeter	Goat owned by Lynda Snell
Lone Ranger	Freda Fry's stray cat who died from what appeared to be a snake bite in 2007
Persephone	Goat owned by Lynda Snell
Salieri	Constanza and Wolfgang's llama baby
Sammy	Peggy's cat
Wolfgang	Constanza's llama mate (now deceased)

The 1980s Brookfield pig unit at Hollowtree was made up of a lively bunch of boars: Playboy I, II and III, Cromwell, Monty and Hercules

• QUIZ NIGHT AT THE BULL •

WHAT'S FOR DINNER?

1. What party food did Susan Carter forbid son Christopher from eating at the opening of the Dan Archer Memorial Children's Playground in 1996?

2. Which Glebe Cottage resident tried and failed to make marmalade in 2009 when the jam thermometer snapped off in the pan?

3. Name the Birmingham takeaway where Usha Franks bought Indian food to feed to the women of the WI.

4. After travelling to India, what was Freda Fry inspired to make?

5. Pat Archer was stirring a pan of what when she finally broke down after John's death?

6. Who was the unlikely writer of a cookery column for the *Borchester Echo*?

7. Mrs Scroby claims adding mustard to beer, boiling it and drinking it is a cure for what?

8. What kind of cake competition did Grey Gables chef Jean-Paul judge in 1999?

9. Who went on the 'within five miles' diet for Lent in 2009?

10. Whose wedding reception in 1957 featured the revolutionary idea of a buffet rather than a sit-down meal?

11. Which centrepiece dish fell spectacularly apart at Rob and Jess Titchener's ill-fated Christmas party?

12. What did Brian do after eating Kate's vegan Easter meal?

MEMORABLE MOMENTS:
LILIAN DISCOVERING MATT'S GONE

Date: 15 January 2015
Location: The Dower House

Pusscat and Tiger have had plenty of ups and downs: affairs, fraud, prison, lies. But none of us, especially not Lilian, were prepared for that cold bleak day in January 2015 when she returned from holiday and found Matt gone. Vanished. With the paintings taken from the walls and the safe hanging half open, Lilian was justified in thinking that she had been burgled. But a two-word note – 'Sorry, Pusscat' – left her sadly in no doubt what had happened. Though Matt was a rogue, he was usually lovable with it, so it was difficult to imagine him selling the family silver and leaving Lilian in the lurch so horribly. We suspect that if she had only come home a little earlier than planned, in time to catch him, it would all have played out differently. Matt would never have departed in such a dastardly way in front of her. 'Tiger, what are you doing?' 'Oh, you're back early from your holiday, Pusscat. Err, just taking the paintings down for a closer look...' Matt never could resist Lilian's husky tones and sexy laugh, and that's why he left when she wasn't there, so he wouldn't be tempted to stay. He will be sadly missed. As will Lilian's sexy laugh – when will we hear it again? Listeners expressed their sympathy for Lilian on Twitter: @Lindabell15 said: 'Oh Lilian, it's all very well to stand by your man and all that but HE'S TAKEN THE WINE!' And @valj48 agreed: 'Catch him if you can (and make him pay) it's time to break free! Matt the leopard hasn't changed his spots!'

WELCOME TO AMBRIDGE: HONEYSUCKLE COTTAGE

- As one of the most picturesque cottages in Ambridge, thatched Honeysuckle overlooks the duck pond and the village green.
- Deathwatch beetle was discovered in the thatch in 1977.
- A small pile of stones in the garden marks the grave of Nelson Gabriel's daughter's dog Winston.
- The house was refurbished and extended by previous residents Tim and Siobhan Hathaway.
- The house is currently occupied by Adam Macy and his civil partner Ian Craig and has its own hot tub.

MEET THE CHARACTERS: ALAN AND USHA FRANKS

Usha Gupta became partner at Mark Hebden's Borchester law practice in 1991. She had a rocky few years in Ambridge, including being targeted by racists, and her former friend Shula sleeping with her partner Richard. But meeting new vicar Alan changed her life. He was a widower with a daughter, Amy. Eyebrows were raised about their relationship, particularly when it was noted that a statue of the Hindu God Shiva had appeared in the vicarage living room. Alan was summoned to see the bishop following written complaints from three parishioners. However, the bishop was very supportive, which is more than can be said for Usha's parents, her interfering Aunt Satya, and Alan's mother-in-law Mabel. Despite the opposition, Alan and Usha married in 2008, and over the years their strong marriage has managed to bring round most people. Not Shula, of course, who resigned from her role as churchwarden. She and Usha still struggle to be civil to each other.

DID YOU KNOW?

- Alan and Usha had two weddings: a Hindu one first, then a Christian one two days later.
- Usha's brother Shiv is an accountant.
- Usha and Amy fell out over Amy's married boyfriend, but made up at Usha's fiftieth birthday party.
- Alan got into hot water with Usha when he presented her with anniversary roses from their garden that she'd been planning to enter in the Flower and Produce Show.

GONE BUT NOT FORGOTTEN:
TOM FORREST

Born: 20 October 1910
Died: 5 November 1998
Played by: Bob Arnold

By the time Tom Forrest was in his forties, his sister Doris Archer and most of his friends had resigned themselves to his bachelor ways. For years he had worked as a gamekeeper, following in the footsteps of his father, William, and found pleasure in the simple things – bell-ringing, singing and the warm welcome he always received at Brookfield Farm. It came as quite a shock then when he took a shine to Bull barmaid Pru Harris after acting as executor of her mother's will; the two struck up a close friendship.

It took the dramatic events of Ned Larkin's brother Bob arriving in Ambridge to bring them closer together. When Bob proposed to Pru, Tom was furious and the two exchanged harsh words. Then when Tom found Bob poaching, there was a tussle, and Bob's gun accidentally went off, killing him. Tom went on trial for manslaughter but was acquitted by the jury – he arrived back in Ambridge to a hero's welcome and the sound of the Hollerton Silver Band playing 'For He's a Jolly Good Fellow'. This trying time led to him proposing to Pru and their wedding in September 1958.

Though they met later in life, the couple spent a happy 37 years together, mainly living at Keeper's Cottage, built for them by Charles Grenville. They fostered two boys in their time together – Johnny Martin and Peter Stevens – and Tom worked as Sporting Manager for Jack Woolley, and after trying to retire found himself managing Jack's garden centre and fishery. In later life they moved into The Laurels nursing home together. Tom Forrest – the man who loved biscuits, bell-ringing and kept the friendly competition of the Flower and Produce Show alive with his rivalry with Bert Fry – died a week after his beloved wife Pru. Their names are both inscribed on bells in St Stephen's Church tower.

LISTENER PORTRAIT

When and why did you start listening? When I was a schoolboy, circa 1974. It was when I discovered Radio 4 and I remember it took me a bit of time to acquire the taste of listening to *The Archers*.

What's your most memorable Ambridge moment? When Walter Gabriel was banned from The Bull (but I can't remember why).

Which character would you most like to meet? Kenton Archer – especially as I recently learnt that the person who acts the part lives near me!

Which character drives you crazy? Lilian can come close – especially when she was going out with Paul.

The Archers **is wonderful because...** all human life is contained in its sound world.

Philip Willat, former Director of Human Resources

QUIZ NIGHT AT THE BULL

LOVE IS IN THE AIR!

1. Whose wedding were David Archer and Sophie Barlow watching on TV when he proposed to her?

2. Who took Caroline Bone to London for a secret romantic getaway in 1985?

3. Kathy Perks embraced the singles dating scene at a dinner party where she met Richard who was an expert in which piece of office equipment?

4. What kind of ring did David Archer present to his wife Ruth for Christmas in 2000?

5. Name the man who kept his options open in the 1980s by sending Valentine's cards to Shula, Elizabeth and Jill?

6. When her family moved north in 1959 what did Joan Hood give Jimmy Grange as a token of her undying love?

7. Mike Tucker was taken to the theatre by lonely hearts match Wendy. What play did they see?

8. In 1986 a Grey Gables guest from Santa Barbara called Patience Talt was proposed to by which Ambridge resident?

9. Who received a device for scraping ice off a car windscreen from her new husband for Christmas?

10. Who was romanced by handsome wine importer Robin Fairbrother and his BMW?

11. Where were Adam and Ian on holiday in January 2015 when they decided they would have a proper wedding, in addition to their civil ceremony?

12. Which park did Matt and Lilian take a romantic carriage ride round?

MAKING THE ARCHERS:
AMBRIDGE HAS THE
EXTRA-FACTOR

In 2011, the BBC announced that they were going to broadcast a new spin-off programme on BBC Radio 4 Extra called *Ambridge Extra*. The digital station aired two episodes of the programme on Thursdays at 10 a.m., with repeated episodes at 2.15 p.m. Half-hour omnibus editions were aired on Fridays and Sundays. The new show was designed to mark the sixtieth anniversary year of *The Archers*. Editor Vanessa Whitburn described *Ambridge Extra* as a bonus for listeners who wanted to spend more time immersed in the lives of the Ambridge characters. While *The Archers* has always been written as a continuous drama with five, and later six, episodes airing each week, *Ambridge Extra* was planned as a finite series with only two episodes a week, and would therefore focus on a smaller number of characters and fewer storylines.

Over the next two years there were five series of *Ambridge Extra*, before it was 'rested'. It's uncertain whether it will return in future. The first series (26 episodes) focused on Alice and her misguided dalliance with her university housemate, 'Chaz'. The second (26 episodes) mainly revolved round Daniel and his girlfriend Erin, and her slightly unlikely interest in Dan's stepfather Alistair. This series featured the never-before-heard (and quickly abandoned) device of hearing the characters' thoughts, which was disturbing and confusing in equal part. It was light relief, therefore, to turn to the other focus of this series, Clive Horrobin being vaguely menacing to Amy Franks. Series 3 (20 episodes) was the most well-travelled, adhering to the original promise of *Ambridge Extra* that it would venture further afield than Ambridge. We heard Kate and Phoebe in South Africa, Jolene and Kenton in Australia, and Fallon, Harry and Jazzer in a broken-down van in Cumbria. Series 4 (20 episodes) headed to the dark side of Ambridge, with storylines centering on Tracy and Bert Horrobin, and a sideline of trouble between Alan and Usha. Series 5 (10 episodes, though it felt longer) was the craziest of all, with Matt and Brenda running wild in St Petersburg, getting in the way of Russian mafia plots, and being rescued by Bond Girl Lilian.

The makers of the show were keen to stress that *Archers* fans could still listen to the original programme as a stand-alone series without missing key plot developments. However, one or two of the series did have plot points that listeners felt were too important to have only in an 'optional' programme. Those who heard *Ambridge Extra* (approximately 250,000 listeners each week), certainly had an advantage when events which were briefly alluded to in the main programme had been explored in detail in *Extra*. Overall, however, it was generally felt that after a shaky start, the programme definitely added something to the depth of the characters, and made for an enjoyable supplement to the world of *The Archers*.

WELCOME TO AMBRIDGE:
KEEPER'S COTTAGE AND APRIL COTTAGE

- This pair of three-bedroom cottages was built in 1960 by Charles Grenier. They are situated not far from Ambridge Hall.
- Initially Keeper's Cottage was built to provide accommodation for Charles's workers after the original workers' cottages were demolished to make way for a new road.
- Former Keeper's Cottage resident, Tom Forrest, helped decide the layout of the house when it was being built and developed the garden into the home for Pru's many prize-winning Flower and Produce Show entries.
- John Archer moved into April Cottage with Hayley Jordan (now Tucker) in early 1997, and it was where she later caught him cheating on her with ex-love Sharon Richards.
- Current occupants of April Cottage are Kathy Perks and her son Jamie, while Keeper's Cottage is home to Joe, Eddie and Clarrie Grundy. Both cottages were damaged by the floods, and to Clarrie's horror, she discovered that their contents weren't insured.

MEET THE CHARACTERS: THE ARCHERS OF BRIDGE FARM

Tony and Pat have weathered a great many crises over the years. Neither really recovered fully from son John's untimely death. But they have also had to cope with an outbreak of E. coli which almost brought their business to its knees, the suicide of Helen's partner Greg, Tom's abandonment of Kirsty at the altar, and Tony's run-in with Otto the bull which left him hospitalised for weeks. But they plod on stoically.

Neither Tom nor Helen could be said to be lucky in love. Helen's first proper relationship, with brooding gamekeeper Greg Turner, ended tragically when he took his own life in 2004. Later there was Leon, who slept with (and impregnated) Greg's daughter Annette, who was Helen's housemate at the time. And then there was Rob, whose dark side Helen seems unable to see. Tom's not done much better. Devastated when fiancée Brenda left him, Tom found solace in the arms of Kirsty, whom he had chucked many years earlier. But he dumped her again, this time making it miles worse by waiting till they were in the church on their actual wedding day. Helen at least has found fulfilment in her son Henry, born by donor insemination in 2010.

The newest arrival to Bridge Farm is Johnny Phillips, the son of John and Sharon, whose existence wasn't known to the Archers until the boy was in his teens. His farm skills seem to come naturally and he is a source of great comfort to Tony and Pat.

DID YOU KNOW?

- Tony Archer lost his job as a dairy manager for Ralph Bellamy when he skipped work to be with summer school teacher Jane Petrie.
- Pat Archer was once the county champion at javelin.
- John Archer's favourite childhood storybook was *Little Piggly Wiggly* and the song played by Hayley Jordan (now Tucker) at his funeral was 'Wonderwall' by Oasis.
- Helen Archer received six GCSEs and studied for an HND in food technology with management.
- Tom Archer's seventeenth birthday was the same day his brother John died.
- Johnny has difficulty reading and may have dyslexia.

PORTRAIT OF THE WRITER AS LISTENER:

SALLY WAINWRIGHT

Former Archers scriptwriter Sally Wainwright has written for Coronation Street *and other soap operas. She is also the writer of the original series* Last Tango in Halifax *and* Happy Valley, *among others.*

When and why did you start listening? My mum always put it on, she'd listened to it since it started in the 1950s, but even though it was always on in our house, I didn't actually *listen* to it. I started listening to it properly when I was asked to write a trial script for it by Ruth Patterson (the editor). So it felt very familiar to me even though I didn't know who anyone was. My mum gave me a crash course in who all the characters were and all the family connections, and their big story lines.

What's your most memorable Ambridge moment? Eddie Grundy throwing up inside the piano in The Bull. It was an episode written by Paul Burns. It was sublime.

Which character would you most like to meet? My favourite character was always Betty Tucker. I loved writing for Betty. She was a kind, intelligent, broad-shouldered woman.

Which character drives you crazy? David Archer, because he is arrogant and boring. How could Phil and Jill have spawned him? Kenton, Shula and Elizabeth are all multi-layered, interesting characters. I suppose they had to have one dull-as-ditchwater one.

The Archers **is wonderful because...** it never ends.

If you could make one change to *The Archers* it would be... to put it on television.

GONE BUT NOT FORGOTTEN:
SID PERKS

Born: 9 June 1944
Died: 8 June 2010
Played by: Alan Devereux

When Brummie Sid Perks arrived in Ambridge in 1963 fresh out of borstal, he was taken under Jack Woolley's wing and quickly found himself employed as Jack's chauffeur/handyman. He married barmaid Polly, who bought and ran the village shop as postmistress, with Sid's help. After experiencing a miscarriage after a raid at the shop, Polly gave birth to a healthy daughter, Lucy. Sid and Polly then sold up the shop and began running The Bull, where they set about making dramatic improvements – opening a restaurant, offering bed-and-breakfast accommodation and restoring the bowling green.

Polly died tragically in a car accident in 1982, leaving Sid distraught and a single father. He married Lucy's form teacher, Kathy Holland (after three proposals) and so began a tumultuous relationship of affairs (Kathy with Dave Barry and Sid with Jolene Rogers) and arguments. They finally became owners of The Bull in 1993 and had a son, Jamie, in 1995, but their responsibilities were not enough to keep them together and Kathy moved out, making way for new vivacious barmaid Jolene, whom Sid married in 2002. After eight happy years of marriage to Jolene, Sid died of a heart attack while on holiday in New Zealand visiting daughter Lucy. Both Kathy and Jolene felt the loss very deeply, as did Sid and Kathy's son Jamie.

QUIZ NIGHT AT THE BULL

FIELDS AND FARMERS

1. After an outbreak of foot-and-mouth disease in 1956 Dan Archer replaced which breed of cows with Friesians?

2. Which farmer diversified with the introduction of deer and shooting parties in 1987?

3. What business did Mike Tucker start with the compensation money he received after he lost his eye?

4. At which farm was Neil Carter an apprentice?

5. What is the name of the semi-hard cheese Oliver Sterling's Guernsey milk is used to produce?

6. Which estate created Home Farm when parts of it were sold off in the 1970s?

7. What disease was there an outbreak of in Ambridge in 1955?

8. Onto which farm did a German plane crash land during World War Two?

9. In 1951 when Dan Archer bought his first tractor, which of his horses did he sell to Walter Gabriel?

10. The introduction of what in 1984 saw Brookfield reduce its cow herd from 110 to 95?

11. What did Tom convince Pat and Tony to sell, after 35 years at Bridge Farm?

12. Who experimented with planting a herbal ley to improve the soil?

WELCOME TO AMBRIDGE: LOWER LOXLEY HALL

- Home to the Pargetter family for centuries, stately home Lower Loxley Hall, just two miles east of Ambridge, has Jacobean origins but was added to substantially over time as the year 1702, written over the door, indicates.
- Most of the house is open to the public for tours and it also doubles up as a conference centre.
- Guests can enjoy the toy museum in the old nursery, a treetop walk in the arboretum, a visit to the animals in the rare-breeds farm and a high-quality meal from local produce in the Orangery Café. The vineyard produces well-regarded wine which is sold under the Lower Loxley name – a 'nice crisp white' according to the experts at English Wine Lovers. It was awarded Regional Wine Status in 2008.
- Lower Loxley Hall is set in seven acres of picturesque woodland and a further three acres of informal gardens. There is a cycle route around the grounds and visitors are able to hire bikes.

- Lower Loxley plays host to a number of public events to support the running costs of the property, including December's 'Deck the Halls', which has previously featured a German market and an ice rink, and the Easter Egg-Stravaganza in 2006. The most ambitious event to date was the three-day music festival, Loxfest, in August 2014, which was headlined by the Pet Shop Boys. Also on the bill were the Midnight Walkers, featuring vocals from PC Harrison Burns. He was omnipresent at the festival, later mingling with the crowds and being on the spot in time to arrest Fallon's dad, Wayne, mid drug deal.

- Lower Loxley is a popular venue for weddings, and it offers a number of options, including green weddings, which use only local produce.

- Hillside is a two-house development just across the road from Lower Loxley, which was split into flats by property developer Matt Crawford. Milkman Harry Mason was one of the first residents, and he was joined shortly afterwards by flatmate-from-hell Jazzer. Other residents are probably glad that both men have now left, as Jazzer's late-night habits would not have gone unnoticed.

FAMOUS FACES IN AMBRIDGE: PART 3

Think Ambridge is just a place for farming folk and welly boots? Think again! It may not be Hollywood, but the Hassett Hills have seen more famous faces than an Oscars after-party.

★ Celebrity gardener and self-confessed *Archers* fan **Alan Titchmarsh** found himself on the programme in 2003 when he took on the thankless task of judging Ambridge's entry for the National Garden Scheme.

★ July 2004 saw celebrated Welsh comedian and presenter **Griff Rhys Jones** attend a reception at Grey Gables. Snared by the persistent Lynda Snell, he soon found himself recruited into her campaign to restore the Cat and Fiddle pub.

★ While not part of the official programme, comedienne **Victoria Wood**, a dedicated *Archers* fan, wrote a short mini-series for Comic Relief called *Victoria Goes to Ambridge* in 2005 that featured **Stephen Fry, Ewan McGregor, Liza Tarbuck** and **Sir Ian McKellen**. The episodes were aired on Radio 4 with listeners voting for which celebrity they wanted to take the lead role in the final episode (Stephen won). That same week **Chris Moyles** showed up in The Bull ordering a cocktail.

★ Fashion icon and designer **Zandra Rhodes** did her bit to promote stylish ways in Borsetshire when she appeared in a September 2006 fashion show episode. She agreed to appear in the programme without hesitation when she was asked, having been a lifelong fan of *The Archers* ever since the dramatic episode where Grace Archer died in a barn fire.

★ When Sid and Jolene Perks were at Lords Cricket Ground for the npower Village Cup final in 2007, Sid went missing for an hour. When Jolene finally spotted him being led towards an MCC box by none other than former England cricket captain **Mike Gatting**, the anxious landlady gave chase to save her husband from his 'kidnapper'.

★ As one of Britain's leading medical academics, heralded for his research into human fertility, **Professor Robert Winston (Lord Winston)** was more than happy to feature in an *Archers* storyline in his effort to popularise science. In 2007 he played Roy and Hayley Tucker's medical consultant on the programme, who investigated why the couple were having trouble conceiving.

MEET THE CHARACTERS: REX AND TOBY FAIRBROTHER

These two brothers popped up, rather out of the blue, in spring 2015. They wanted to rent a piece of land to start up a geese and duck business. Their decision to move to the area was less random than it initially appeared: their grandfather, George Fairbrother, used to live in Ambridge. George was a landowner in the 1950s, and he had two children, Robin (Rex and Toby's father), and Grace (Phil's first wife). Robin was rather a cad to Elizabeth back in the day. They were seeing each other in the late 1980s, when Elizabeth was 20 and Robin 34, then she found out he was still married. It was all a bit awkward for Jill even before this was discovered, as she was uncomfortable with her daughter dating the half-brother of Phil's first wife (a sort of uncle, if you're following this).

DID YOU KNOW?

- The affair between Elizabeth and Robin Fairbrother ended at Nelson's Wine Bar, when Robin told her he was going back to his wife, and Lizzie poured a glass of wine over his head.

- Rex, the older brother, was a professional rugby player, until his career was brought to a halt by injury.

- Toby used to work in the City, but is also keen on rugby.

- Pip was rather smitten with Toby from their first meeting.

RIP

GONE BUT NOT FORGOTTEN:
JOHN ARCHER

Born: 31 December 1975
Died: 25 February 1998
Played by: Sam Barriscale

While many tragedies have befallen the folk of Ambridge over the years, for Pat and Tony Archer the loss of their eldest son, John, in 1998 was probably their darkest hour. At just 22 years old, things were just getting going for the ambitious youngster who had undertaken a National Diploma in Agriculture at Borchester College and raised his own fully organic pigs. A rebellious older child by nature, John had got off to a rocky start, with only a mild interest in farming. His attentions were more often shared between American football and girls. When teen mum Sharon Richards moved into the caravan at Bridge Farm, his parents thought his infatuation unhealthy and were relieved to pack him off to an agricultural school in Somerset. But his feelings for Sharon didn't abate, and later during his gap year, after a row with his mother about Sharon not taking responsibility for damaging Peggy's van, he stormed out to live with Sharon in her council house. When Sharon left John and Ambridge for Leeds, he was heartbroken and turned to a string of girls to help him move on. Last in line was Hayley Jordan (now Tucker), whom he met at a Birmingham nightclub. Just when things were looking good for John – he was living with Hayley at April Cottage, working for his dad and raising his pigs – Sharon arrived back on the scene and he began an affair with his former girlfriend. Caught red-handed by Hayley, John realised only when she'd left him that he had made a big mistake. When a wedding proposal at the expensive Mont Blanc restaurant wasn't enough to win her back, John was heartbroken.

The next day, on his brother's seventeenth birthday, he headed out in the cabless vintage Ferguson tractor to repair a fence and never came back. His lifeless body was found trapped beneath the tractor by his father Tony. John never knew that Sharon was pregnant with their son, who would, years later, find his way to Ambridge and into Pat and Tony's hearts.

DOWN THE AISLE

St Stephen's Church has seen its fair share of romantic unions, unfortunately not all of them lasting as long as the starry-eyed young lovers may have initially hoped. Weddings in Ambridge have caused controversy, jealousy and a fair bit of drama, and have been nothing if not memorable. Here is a list of some notable *Archers* weddings, both at the church and elsewhere.

1 January 1991	Peggy Archer and Jack Woolley
1 January 2012	Nic Hanson and Will Grundy
1 February 1967	Carol Grenville and John Tregorran
25 February 1984	Susan Horrobin and Neil Carter
1 March 1979	Christine Johnson and George Barford
11 April 1955	Grace Fairbrother and Phil Archer
12 April 2001	Kate Aldridge and Lucas Madikane
24 April 1987	Kathy Holland and Sid Perks
27 August 2004	Emma Carter and Will Grundy
7 May 2001	Hayley Jordan and Roy Tucker
12 May 2000	Debbie Aldridge and Simon Gerrard
22 May 2015	Emma Grundy and Ed Grundy
26 May 1969	Lilian Archer and Lester Nicholson
26 May 2005	Julia Pargetter and Lewis Carmichael
29 May 1976	Jennifer Travers-Macy and Brian Aldridge

30 May 1994	Lucy Perks and Duncan Gemmell
25 June 1972	Betty and Mike Tucker
29 June 1963	Janet Sheldon and John Tregorran
29 June 2006	Caroline Pemberton and Oliver Sterling
4 July 2002	Jolene Rogers and Sid Perks
15 July 2009	Vicky Hudson and Mike Tucker
28 July 2010	Alice Aldridge and Christopher Carter
27 & 29 August 2008	Usha Gupta and Alan Franks (they had a Hindu ceremony followed by a Christian ceremony two days later)
3 September 1971	Lilian Nicholson and Ralph Bellamy
11 September 1995	Caroline Bone and Guy Pemberton
21 September 1985	Shula Archer and Mark Hebden
27 September 1966	Polly Mead and Sid Perks
27 September 1968	Jennifer Archer and Roger Travers-Macy
29 September 1994	Elizabeth Archer and Nigel Pargetter
4 October 2006	Eileen Pugsley and Edgar Titcombe
1 November 2013	Jolene Perks and Kenton Archer
16 November 1957	Jill Patterson and Phil Archer
21 November 1981	Clarrie Larkin and Eddie Grundy
12 December 1974	Pat Lewis and Tony Archer
14 December 2006	Adam Macy and Ian Craig (civil partnership)
15 December 1988	Ruth Pritchard and David Archer
17 December 1921	Doris Forrest and Dan Archer
24 December 1999	Shula Hebden and Alistair Lloyd

LISTENER PORTRAIT

When and why did you start listening? In 1982 I was on an archaeological dig in northern France with my friend Duncan. One day we were on mega washing-up duty and he said let's see if we can get Radio 4. We could and it was *The Archers*. I barely knew what Radio 4 was, and thought it all very strange, but there was something about being abroad and listening to a story of the English countryside that got me hooked. When I got home I found it was on on a Sunday morning and it seemed a good excuse to have a lie in.

What's your most memorable Ambridge moment? It was when Nelson Gabriel tried to seduce David's girlfriend Sophie and she said, 'Nelson, you've got black satin sheets!' I was also quite involved with the plot with Emma going back to Ed – I remember having to listen in a field once when I was camping so as not to miss it.

Which character would you most like to meet? Part of me wants to say Lilian Bellamy because she would be highly entertaining company (this is before Matt left and she became miserable of course), but the truth is that I would probably spend a much better afternoon with one of the more normal characters. Kirsty comes to mind, particularly as she has a lovely voice.

Which character drives you crazy? Too many to count... any child under ten, and Christine Barford, but probably Helen most of all. She is one of those people one just wants to shake.

The Archers **is wonderful because...** How could one resist a programme that had Joe Grundy in it?

If you could make one change to *The Archers* **it would be...** to send Helen on a long sabbatical and replace her with Kirsty.

Trish Joscelyne, psychologist

WELCOME TO AMBRIDGE: NIGHTINGALE FARM

- Nightingale Farm once belonged to Lady Isabel Lander – the wealthy heiress had inherited it from her uncle Brigadier Winstanley.
- When Hugo Barnaby bought the house from Isabel, he used most of the building as a youth club and arts and crafts centre.
- Neil and Susan Carter rented the property from Hugo as their first home together. Later he offered them £4,000 to leave the flat so he could sell it, which they did and moved to No. 1 The Green.
- Nightingale Farm is only a farm by name but was home to Marjorie Antrobus's eight Afghan hounds when she was the owner.
- Currently owned by Matt Crawford, the house has seen a number of tenants, including Ruth Archer and Nigel Pargetter, Richard Locke and Hayley and Roy Tucker, all of whom took their turn as Marjorie's lodgers over the years. Little is known about the current tenant, other than they are an 'incomer'.

• QUIZ NIGHT AT THE BULL •

FARMING FASHIONS

1. After seeing Julia Pargetter on stage in the 1940s and handing her a rose, what gift did her future husband Gerald send to her?

2. Which two women set up a rather unsuccessful fashion business together in the 1980s?

3. Who used to dazzle audiences in fringed and rhinestone-decorated buckskin shirts in his country and western days?

4. Which popular item of clothing does Lynda never wear?

5. Whose party trick used be undoing girls' bras through their clothes?

6. Who presented Shula with a grass skirt when he returned home on leave from the Merchant Navy in 1975?

7. In 1998 Peggy organised a fashion show at Grey Gables. Which store provided the clothes?

8. What item of clothing did Marjorie give to Joe Grundy when he tried lonely hearts dating in the late 1980s?

9. What woolly item did Martha Woodford knit for all the village children?

10. What colour Bo Peep-style dresses did Elizabeth Archer's bridesmaids wear to her wedding to Nigel Pargetter?

11. When the cellar of The Bull flooded in 2014, which of Jolene's belongings were ruined?

12. What surprising item did Joe Grundy like to wear, when the family was staying at Grey Gables during the flood aftermath?

MEET THE CHARACTERS: THE SNELLS

Robert and Lynda were particularly affected by the floods of 2015, losing their much-loved dog Scruff, as well as coping with the damage to their house and garden. Luckily Lynda's pride and joy, her llamas Constanza and Salieri, avoided harm. Robert is a computer software specialist by trade, though since being made redundant he has reinvented himself as Ambridge's 'Mr Fix-It'. Lynda works as the receptionist at Grey Gables, and is also a parish councillor, which fits in nicely along with her unofficial role as general busybody. She is easily the most vocal member of the SAVE campaign, an Ambridge group set up to oppose the plans for the proposed 'Route B' road. And there would be no village shows without Lynda, though there is invariably a moment, mid-rehearsal, when she swears, 'Never again!' But she is usually talked round.

Robert has two daughters, Leonie and Coriander, from his first marriage. Coriander has a son called Oscar whom step-grandma Lynda adores. Leonie visited Ambridge early in 2011 at the same time as Lilian's son James; Lynda and Robert were delighted when the two became an item. When Leonie and James' first child was born, Lynda's delight turned to dismay as they announced they were calling the boy Mowgli. She was relieved when they changed it to the slightly more acceptable Mungo. As with Oscar, Lynda's doting on Mungo knows no bounds.

DID YOU KNOW?

�֎ Robert is a keen cricketer and was snapped up by the village team when they heard he was a member of the MCC.

✖ Lynda's slogan for her 1987 Ambridge Parish Council election campaign was 'Snell for a greener Ambridge'.

✖ Robert's first wife is called Bobo.

✖ Lynda once used the nom de plume Dylan Nells when writing for *Borsetshire Life* magazine.

✖ Unable to have children of her own, Lynda has been the 'mother' of a number of animals in her time: goats, puppies, hedgehogs and even ladybirds.

MAKING THE ARCHERS: DISSECTING 'DUM-DI-DUM'

Even for those people who claim never to have listened to *The Archers*, or even Radio 4, the 'dum-di-dum' opening melody to the programme is widely recognised. The piece of music itself is actually entitled 'Barwick Green' and is a maypole dance from the 1924 suite *My Native Heath* by Yorkshire composer Sir Arthur Wood. The title refers to a village east of Leeds called Barwick-in-Elmet. Sidney Torch conducted the original orchestral recording used to introduce and close the programme from 1950; the theme was re-recorded in stereo in 1992 and an alternative version has also been recorded by Somerset folk band The Yetties for the Sunday omnibus edition of the programme. It's hard to imagine *The Archers* without that memorable tune, but on April Fool's Day in 2004 the *Today* programme ran a story revealing that the theme tune was being updated by ambient music composer Brian Eno. In a very convincing interview, Eno stated that there was only so much 'dum-di-dum' anyone could take in a lifetime, and that *The Archers* wanted to move with the rest of the world into the 21st century. Needless to say, the original theme tune has remained and isn't going anywhere any time soon. In 2011, as part of Radio 3's Light Fantastic festival, amateur musicians were invited to download their instrument's part for 'Barwick Green' and upload a video of them performing it. The resulting performances were mixed to create an online orchestra performance to be broadcast on Radio 3. A year later, it featured in the opening ceremony of the Olympics. So well-loved and embedded in popular culture is the tune that comedian Billy Connolly once suggested it replace 'God Save the Queen' as the British national anthem. And in 2015 Stephen Fry chose it as one of his Desert Island Discs, saying, 'I think if I heard this on my on my desert island, it would take me all the way home.' When folk band Bellowheadre-recorded the tune for *Archers* spin-off programme *Ambridge Extra*, the change was met with scepticism by most fans. The *Guardian* described the new version as sounding like a 'French-themed booze-up on Captain Pugwash's pirate ship'. Sir Arthur is probably turning in his grave.

MEMORABLE MOMENTS:
THE STATE OF ROY'S HOUSE, POST HAYLEY

Date: Various points during early 2015
Location: Willow Farm

Roy rather fell to pieces when Hayley left him (and Elizabeth turned him down). He just about managed to keep it together at work, but it was at home – now emptied of his family – that really bore the brunt of his decline. We first heard about the state of the place through Tom, though he was in no position to judge about messy lives. But then Lynda went round there collecting for the jumble sale, and was appalled at what she saw. A week or so later (and how much worse it must have got in that time – congealing pizza crusts, the brown apple cores, sticky marks from beer bottles, discarded socks), Phoebe turned up. Though a teenager, even she was horrified: it must have been bad. Then Kate barged in, and had the cheek to tell Roy that he couldn't see Phoebe until he sorted himself out. Even more mortifyingly, Hayley came round 'to talk', prompting Roy to move a few items around so she could sit down. We could picture her trying to avoid touching anything as she perched on the edge of the sofa. Awful. It seemed like pretty much everyone witnessed the physical evidence of Roy's deterioration, but it wasn't until Mike finally bothered to visit his son that anyone offered to help. By now it had been weeks, and when Mike told Roy to get washed and dressed while he tidied up, we all breathed a huge sigh of relief.

WELCOME TO AMBRIDGE: RICKYARD COTTAGE

- This tiny cottage behind the rick yard on Brookfield Farm was described by herdsman Graham Collard as too small to swing a cat.
- Once a workers' cottage, it has been the home of Simon and Bess Cooper, Ned and Mabel Larkin and Tony Archer in the 1970s.
- It was reverted into a home for Brookfield Farm workers – Mike Tucker lived there, followed by Graham Collard and his wife Val who both moved out in 1991.
- Lisa and Craig found the cottage the ideal place to squat in 1992; it was later turned to profitable use as a holiday let.
- Rickyard was home to Ed and Emma Grundy, but when they couldn't pay the rent they had to move out. It then went back to being used as a holiday let.

LISTENER PORTRAIT

When and why did you start listening? It was in the background as a child – my mother has been listening since the beginning – and then more consistently from about 1992, when I left art college and set up a studio and started default Radio 4 as background.

What's your most memorable Ambridge moment? Susan Carter going down.

Which character would you most like to meet? Jazzer.

Which character drives you crazy? Currently the new Pip Archer – middle-aged and unfeasible.

If you could make one change to *The Archers* it would be... stop making people act out of character for plot devices, e.g. David Archer over the potential move. The unrealistic thing was not his reversal of decision but the frailty of the notion that he would have so easily decided to move in the first place.

Nicholas Lees, artist

QUIZ NIGHT AT THE BULL

OUT OF TOWN

1. At which station did Phil Archer propose to Jill Patterson?

2. In which Borsetshire village is The Half Moon pub?

3. What does Bentham's in Borchester sell?

4. Where was the salsa club that Ruth Archer and Usha Gupta (now Franks) attended?

5. What's the name of the gay bar in Borchester?

6. There used to be a business in Borchester called Sidney's – what was it?

7. What kind of food does Borchester's El Dorado bar/restaurant serve?

8. What is Penny Hassett's Sundial House?

9. Borchester is twinned with a town in which country?

10. How many miles is Ambridge from Felpersham?

11. Which village choral society organised the singing of the Messiah at St Stephen's?

12. Where is the nearest railway station to Ambridge?

RIP

GONE BUT NOT FORGOTTEN:

MARTHA WOODFORD

Born: 31 July 1922
Died: 17 January 1996
Played by: Mollie Harris

Thank goodness for Martha Woodford working at the village shop – without her, Ambridge's residents would never have kept on top of all the gossip and goings-on in the village. This Penny Hassett lass had once been married to postman Herbert Lily and arrived in the village as a widow in 1970 to work part-time in the Ambridge Hall field studies centre. Not shy of getting her hands dirty, she took on cleaning work for Doris Archer and scrubbed away at The Bull. Perhaps tiring of doing other people's dirty work, she saw her life take a new turn in 1972 when she married forestry expert Joby Woodford and approached Jack Woolley about working in the village shop. After an initial refusal, and a brief post at Ralph Bellamy's garage, she began working for Jack and took over from Angela Cooper as manager. She introduced an off-licence section and home delivery service and even considered buying the shop when Jack briefly put it on the market.

Martha's marriage to Joby, and their life together at April Cottage, was relatively happy. And even though it was too late for them to start a family, they opened their home up to farming apprentice Neil Carter, whom they came to regard as a son. After Joby's death in 1993, Martha remained single, although she did take full advantage of the attentions of Joe Grundy and Bill Insley, by getting them to fix her garden gate and chop her firewood. She left her managerial role at the shop in 1989 and stayed on part-time, supporting new boss Betty Tucker through the ordeal of an armed raid in 1993. In January

1996 the little birds of Ambridge must not have known whom to turn to with their twitterings of gossip when Bert Fry found Martha dead in her garden holding a bunch of snowdrops in her hand.

MEET THE CHARACTERS: FALLON ROGERS AND PC HARRISON BURNS

The beginning of their relationship was somewhat will-they-won't-they, but Fallon finally succumbed to Harrison's law-abiding charms. She even forgave him (eventually) for arresting her no-good father, Wayne, for dealing drugs at Loxfest. Fallon has for some time been moving towards a portfolio career, juggling bar-work and vintage party catering with upcycling old furniture. Her dream job would be to run her own tearoom, and this nearly became a reality when Kenton thought he was about to inherit his share of Brookfield.

Harrison was the hero of the hour during the Ambridge floods, as he was the first to realise that the waters were rising dangerously high, and got people to safety before it was too late. He is extremely visible for a local bobby, and seems to be allocated to absolutely every crime in the vicinity.

DID YOU KNOW?

✂ Fallon is named after a character from TV soap *Dynasty*.

✂ Harrison used to sing with a Smiths tribute band. Jolene was impressed enough by this to invite him to join her and the Midnight Walkers at Loxfest.

✤ Fallon's band was called Little White Lies.

✤ Fallon and Jazzer shared a kiss, and rather more, in the van on their way to Scotland (heard only by lucky *Ambridge Extra* listeners).

✤ Fallon's had a few serious relationships, including with Ed Grundy and Rhys Williams, the former barman at The Bull, but maybe Harrison will be The One.

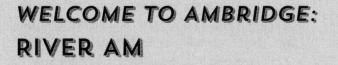

WELCOME TO AMBRIDGE: RIVER AM

✤ Ambridge gets its name from the River Am, which runs through the idyllic Am Vale to Borchester.

✤ Philologists believe the river was originally named the Ambra – this pre-Saxon Celtic word means 'water'.

✤ Other waterways in Borsetshire include the River Mercer, the River Perch and the Felpersham Canal.

�֍ Properties located near the river include Ambridge Hall, Brookfield Bungalow, Nightingale Farm, Glebelands and the Vicarage. In March 2015 the inhabitants of these homes didn't feel so blessed by their idyllic setting when the Am burst its banks and flooded the lower half of the village. Other places affected included April Cottage and Keeper's Cottage, The Green, the riding stables and vet's surgery, The Bull and the village shop. Thankfully, there were very few casualties, other than poor Freda Fry, whose car got stuck in the flood. She was freed by Alan and taken to hospital, but sadly she died ten days later. Charlie Thomas nearly came a cropper, as he got his foot stuck in a drain while trying to clear it, but was rescued by Adam and suffered no more damage than a broken ankle. Suspicions of foul play arose some time later, when it was suggested that someone had deliberately blocked this drain to prevent flooding to Berrow Farm. There were a few animal losses: Home Farm lost 20 sheep and 8 lambs, while Lynda's dog Scruff went missing and is now presumed dead.

FARMER DRAMA

The Archers may be an everyday story of country folk, but that doesn't mean Ambridge is free from the drama, disaster and freak farming accidents that happen in the real world. In more than 60 years and over 17,500 episodes those good country folk have been witness to, and part of, all kinds of drama.

1955

When ITV launched as a brand new channel (a commercial rival to BBC broadcasting) on 22 September, they were faced with tough competition from *The Archers* when Grace Archer – Phil's pretty new bride – found herself trapped in a burning stable and died. In 2008 the BBC released confidential documents that revealed Grace's death was a deliberate move by the BBC to steal viewers from ITV and that it had worked. Grace's death made the front page of the papers and was broadcast to eight million listeners.

1957

Hearing Tom Forrest's struggle with poacher Bob Larkin as the two scrambled about before a shotgun went off was the power of radio drama at its best. Who fired the gun? Who was hurt? Luckily, Tom Forrest survived the fight, the shooting and the ensuing manslaughter trial that followed. But the intervening period was fraught with tension, poignancy and some truly tear-jerking scenes.

1963

Those Borsetshire country roads are no stranger to traffic accidents, but this one was pretty horrific. After John Tregorran finally moved on from his feelings for Carol Grenville and married Janet, she was taken from him four months later when Carol's husband Charles Grenville gave her a lift and they were involved in a serious car accident. Charles lost his leg, but Janet lost her life.

1969

Polly Perks had a miscarriage after a shocking raid on the village post office where she worked.

1972

When an RAF plane crashed in the local area, the whole village helped to hunt for survivors.

1974

Tom and Pru Forrest found George Barford semi-conscious after he had attempted to kill himself by taking an overdose of sleeping pills. Luckily, he survived and soon found himself living with Nora McAuley, who moved in to take care of him.

1982

Those dreaded rural roads caused havoc once again when Polly Perks's life came to an abrupt end. Driving to the cash and carry with Pat Archer, the car skidded on a bend in the road and hit a milk tanker sideways on, killing Polly instantly.

1989

While campaigning to be a local councillor, Brian Aldridge was canvassing the Grundys when he pushed Joe out of the way of a cow suffering with BSE, subsequently being kicked in the head himself. After an operation to remove a blood clot and cerebral abscess, he suffered from post-traumatic epilepsy.

1992

The effects of Elizabeth Archer's abortion were felt throughout her family. After boyfriend Cameron Fraser disappeared from Ambridge, Elizabeth was left devastated and pregnant and despite her mother's protests went through with an abortion. Shula was distressed to discover what her sister had done, as she and husband Mark had been unsuccessfully trying for a baby themselves.

1993

An armed raid on the village shop saw Betty, Debbie, Jack and Kate held hostage by Clive Horrobin and his friend Bruno Wills.

2000

When Ruth Archer found a lump in her breast which turned out to be malignant she underwent a mastectomy and a punishing course of chemotherapy to beat the disease. Listeners were privy to Ruth's fear of leaving her children motherless and her struggle to be intimate with David after the ordeal.

2004

After befriending the quiet chef Owen King during the village production of *A Christmas Carol*, Kathy Perks was left shattered after he attacked and raped her and then acted as if nothing had happened. When she finally told ex-husband Sid what had happened, he scared Owen into leaving Ambridge for good. She did not go to the police until 2007 after learning Owen had attacked another woman.

2010

Her family may not have approved, but that didn't stop Helen Archer going ahead with her sperm-donor pregnancy. With mum Pat's full support she gave birth to Henry Archer on 2 January 2011.

2011

Nigel Pargetter took to the roof of Lower Loxley to remove a New Year's banner, despite icy conditions. He ended up falling from the roof to his death while David Archer watched helplessly. This storyline was part of *The Archers* sixtieth anniversary episode and was widely discussed in the media in the build-up and aftermath.

2012

A gang of thieves beat up Adam when he interrupted them mid-robbery near the polytunnels at Home Farm. Adam was left with a head trauma serious enough that he was unconscious for several days. David, a witness, was then harassed and threatened when he planned to testify against the perpetrators in court, and his barn was set alight. Inevitably, it turned out that there was a Horrobin behind this incident: Keith (Clive and Susan's sister) was part of the gang. He was jailed for four years for arson.

2013

Matt found out about Lilian's steamy affair with his half-brother Paul, although he didn't let on. He sent round one of his henchmen to 'encourage' Paul to stay away from Lilian, and although no violence was involved, it terrified Paul. He died not long after from a heart attack, leaving Lilian devastated and her relationship with Matt in tatters.

2014

Tom decided he couldn't go through with his marriage to Kirsty, but left it rather late to tell her: in the vestry of St Stephen's, with Kirsty wearing one of her two wedding dresses. Kirsty went on their honeymoon without Tom, and he ran off to Canada.

2015

The sudden floods, caused by a combination of torrential rain, high rivers and saturated land, took everyone by surprise. A number of houses were left completely uninhabitable, with people staying with friends, relatives, or at the welcoming surroundings of Grey Gables.

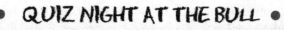

• QUIZ NIGHT AT THE BULL •

WISH YOU WERE HERE!

1. Where did John Tregorran travel to in 1964 to get over the death of his wife Janet?

2. Which of Sid Perks's wives got to go to Nashville for their honeymoon?

3. Which European destination did Jack and Peggy head to in May 1966?

4. Who almost travelled to Ethiopia in the 1950s with the eccentric Lady Hylberow?

5. What crime occurred at Brookfield while Dan and Doris Archer were holidaying in Ireland?

6. Which couple headed to Bali for their honeymoon?

7. When Jennifer and Brian Aldridge became frustrated with the delays to the Home Farm swimming pool, where did they jet off to?

8. Who took their children to the Isle of Man for a holiday in 1968?

9. What did Phil Archer shrink in the wash while Jill was on holiday in Sidmouth?

10. Who embarked on a sailing holiday in 1958?

11. Where did Alice Aldridge and Chris Carter get married?

12. After being jilted by Tom, Kirsty went off on their planned honeymoon with a friend – where?

PORTRAIT OF THE JOURNALIST AS A LISTENER:

HELEN WALMSLEY-JOHNSON

Helen Walmsley-Johnson writes the Invisible Woman column in the Guardian, *and is author of the book* The Invisible Woman: Taking On The Vintage Years.

When and why did you start listening? I've spent the last 15 years living and working in London, which is tough on a country girl. I started listening to *The Archers* because it had the familiar feel of my old rural life and before I knew it Sunday morning had to include my weekly fix of tractors and pigs, silage and gossip. I've come back home to Rutland now – perhaps *The Archers* had something to do with that.

What's your most memorable Ambridge moment? Kirsty's (entirely justified) meltdown at her non-wedding with Tom had me cheering from my kitchen table. I also cheered on Brenda and her reinvention as a high-flying executive assistant because that storyline resonated with me. The best comedic moments are the less obvious ones, like the to-do over Jennifer's fish kettle, or Susan and Clarrie gossiping over yoghurt bottling. The animal sound effects provoke a lot of giggling but that might just be me.

Which character would you most like to meet? Only one? I would like to meet Jennifer's kitchen (without Jennifer in it) because it seems to have assumed an identity all of its own. I want to sit Ed down and give him some coaching in self-esteem and dealing with his loathsome brother. Likewise Helen, who's behaving like a complete idiot over Rob Titchener (also loathsome). Having said that, right at this moment the person I most want to have a chat with is Lilian: after Matt, and Botox notwithstanding, the poor love has a stiff upper lip as rigid as the Hoover dam. I'll bring the gin.

MEET THE CHARACTERS: THE FRYS

Bert and Freda's long and happy marriage sadly came to an end in 2015, with Freda's death. Well known for cooking traditional English pub grub at The Bull, quiet Freda will be much missed. Bert and Freda's son Trevor and daughter-in-law Barbara have a daughter, Amy, whom Bert doted on when she was a child.

DID YOU KNOW?

✂ Bert had his 15 minutes in the spotlight after Elizabeth Archer wrote about his poetic skills in the *Borchester Echo*. He was even asked to be on regional television programme *In Your Corner* to show off his talent.

✂ Bert was strongly opposed to having a woman vicar at St Stephens's when Janet Fisher first arrived.

✂ Freda played the fairy in the 1998 village production of *Jack and the Beanstalk*.

✂ Freda's favourite film was *Guys and Dolls*.

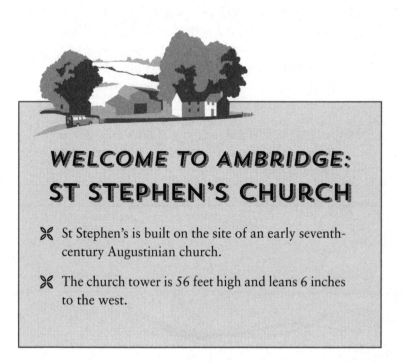

WELCOME TO AMBRIDGE:
ST STEPHEN'S CHURCH

✂ St Stephen's is built on the site of an early seventh-century Augustinian church.

✂ The church tower is 56 feet high and leans 6 inches to the west.

✻ The font is decorated with carved human heads and flowers and is thought to be a gift to the church from Edward I.

✻ A plaque in the church commemorates a peal rung in 1896 that lasted for 3 hours and 20 minutes.

✻ There is a window in the church dedicated to the memory of Grace Archer.

✻ In 1992 building work for a ramp and toilet revealed ancient timbers which were removed for carbon dating.

✻ The church has attracted its fair share of wildlife over the years, including flittermice bats in 1976, a swarm of bees who set up camp near one of the bells and mice who ate their way through the organ stops. The current occupants are a peregrine family that nest in the tower.

✻ During the 2015 floods, the church was one of the key buildings used as a refuge and community centre.

QUIZ NIGHT AT THE BULL

NEW LIFE, NEW STRIFE

1. Which of Clarrie Grundy's sons was two weeks overdue?

2. Before Christine and Paul Johnson adopted Peter, they almost adopted a baby from which country?

3. Who gave birth to her first baby in a tent at the Glastonbury Festival?

4. Coriander Snell was conceived after her parents ate a particularly good meal – but what kind of cuisine was it?

5. Who gave Ruairi Donovan their grandfather's fob watch as a christening present?

6. What condition did Emma Carter have when she was born in 1994?

7. Who left a cricket match against Edgeley two runs short of a half-century in 1997 to make it to the birth of his son?

8. Helen Archer was born breech and with a dislocation of which joint?

9. Who was born with a cleft lip and palate in 1988?

10. Which Archer was born in Australia at 6.20 a.m. on Friday 11 May 2001?

11. What is the name of Jess Titchener's controversial baby?

12. Which baby was born with Down's syndrome in 2013?

RIP

GONE BUT NOT FORGOTTEN:
GRACE ARCHER

Born: 2 April 1929
Died: 22 September 1955
Played by: Ysanne Churchman

Although Grace spent only a few years on the programme, her death remains one of *The Archers'* most talked-about storylines. Grace Fairbrother, the spoilt, beautiful and somewhat coquettish only child of George Fairbrother, caught the attention of Phil Archer straight away. From her arrival in Ambridge she got stuck in with the social scene, promoting the tennis club and becoming secretary of the Young Farmers. Before Grace found herself standing at the altar with Phil, she dallied with the likes of Korean War veteran Alan Carey and the Squire's nephew Clive Lawson-Hope, both of whom proposed, but she got jealous when Phil started dating chicken keeper Jane Maxwell. She even went so far as to find Jane a suitable replacement for Phil, just to stop them becoming more serious. Grace's money and position were a concern to Phil, who eventually proposed but insisted on making money through a pig-breeding scheme before they wed. Tired of waiting, and unsuited to the farming lifestyle, Grace left for Ireland and a year of equestrian training. On her return she was cornered by Phil and agreed to marry him; the couple finally tied the knot on Easter Monday of 1955.

Signs of incompatibility were beginning to show early on when Grace expressed a desire to wait before they had children, while Phil was keen to start a family right away. But the future of the couple was cruelly cut short when a stable fire at Grey Gables claimed Grace's life. She had returned to the burning barn to save Christine Barford's horse and became trapped under a fallen beam. She died in Phil's arms on the way to the hospital, leaving listeners shocked and saddened and the future of the Archer family uncertain.

MAKING THE ARCHERS:
'EASTENDERS-IFICATION'

In early 2015 there was much talk regarding the increase in sensational storylines. Though for many the rot set in with Nigel's death in 2011, most of those who objected to the changes placed the blame squarely at the door of editor Sean O'Connor. Mr O'Connor, who took over the role from Vanessa Whitburn in 2013, had previously been a producer on *EastEnders*. There were those who felt that he had brought an *EastEnders* sensibility to the programme, and that the plot was now 'one damn thing after another'. Fans of the programme waded into the debate. Politician David Blunkett complained that the plot twists were making him 'lose the will to live', while Nancy Banks-Smith, writing in the *Guardian*, went up a soap-level, comparing the newly dramatic *Archers* to *Dallas*, and asked plaintively if 'everyone in the village is on ecstasy'. Even the director-general of the BBC, Tony Hall, felt obliged to comment, saying that he hoped *The Archers* team ensure that 'we don't lose what is precious'.

It's certainly true that lately it's been harder to keep up if you miss a few episodes. Gone are the days when you could stop listening for a couple of years, then check back in and be up to speed within a few minutes. Now, if you go on holiday for a week, you're likely to come back to find Ambridge awash with paternity tests, people changing their minds about selling their farms, jilted brides, rampaging bulls, marriage breakups and people doing runners to Costa Rica. Indeed, you may find Ambridge literally awash, with floods that see off people, pets and great swathes of village infrastructure.

And yet. Listeners with long memories will recall that Grace Archer's death in 1955 was deliberately timed to coincide with, and spoil, the launch of ITV. *The Archers* has never been immune to a certain amount of sensationalism for the sake of listening figures. It has always been a soap of peaks and troughs, though those who have complained of 'sexing up' might not want to admit it. For every slack few weeks in which little more happens than a new outbreak of bovine TB, there are flurries of edge-of-the-seat excitement: Cameron Fraser making a fool of Lizzie; armed robbery in the village shop; John Archer's dramatic death; Sid and Jolene in the shower; Joe bludgeoning the ferrets to death; Brian's affair and subsequent illegitimate child; Greg Turner's suicide; Ruth nearly running off with Sam the herdsman. At heart, *The Archers* is a drama, and dramatic things therefore need to happen. What *The Archers* does so well – and it has never stopped doing it – is taking the long view. Some of its storylines take literally years to come to a head, and there are still plenty of those bubbling away nicely in the background. So perhaps there have been a few more thrilling events than usual lately, but what *The Archers* will never lose is its human touch, and its ability to keep us coming back for more.

WELCOME TO AMBRIDGE: THE BULL

- The Bull is a black-and-white half-timbered building residing near the village green. Traditional Shires ale is served alongside home-cooked food.
- Jack and Peggy Archer paid £5,300 for The Bull when they bought it in 1959.
- Sid and Polly Perks took over as landlords of the pub in 1972, but it wasn't until 1993 that Sid owned the property, buying it from Peggy for £250,000 with the help of investment from Guy Pemberton. It's now run by Jolene and Kenton Archer, and owned jointly by Jolene and Lilian. Kenton had plans to buy out Lilian's share, but these fell through when David decided not to sell Brookfield, thus depriving him of his share of the money.
- In 1995 Kathy Perks revamped The Bull's restaurant with a Civil War theme. On the menu were syllabub, humble pie and Cromwell pudding. Freda Fry presided over the kitchen for many years, and her death in 2015 left a hard-to-fill gap. (Though also an opportunity for a slightly more ambitious menu.)

✕ Landlady Jolene Archer has had a number of money-spinning ideas for the pub, including the cyber-café, a midweek carvery and using the function room as 'The Bull Upstairs' for special music nights. She and husband Kenton sometimes have clashing notions. For instance, for Valentine's night 2014, Kenton organised a romantic dinner for couples downstairs, while Jolene presided over a rather more edgy 'singles night' upstairs.

✕ There are two bars – the public bar and the slightly more upmarket Ploughman's bar. However, at the time of writing, pub patrons are enjoying the spartan comforts of the 'Flood Bar' upstairs, because of the flood damage caused to the main bar.

✕ A pet peacock called Eccles lives in the beer garden.

 LISTENER PORTRAIT

When and why did you start listening? Really before I was conscious. I must have been one or two: the late 1960s. It was put on at the start of bath time and used as a timer for the end of the bath – a perfect 12 minutes.

When our son Max was born, we did the same with him. Ten years on, whenever any of us hears the theme tune, we have a Pavlovian response and say in singsong tones: 'Time to get out!' The omnibus podcast has cemented the programme in my life, and I try to use it as a palliative to insomnia. Though actually, it's often not very soothing these days as a Sunday-night sedative.

Which character would you most like to meet? I wrote to Walter Gabriel as a child, part of a school project. I got a four-page reply, and a black and white snap of Walter and his dog. Very impressive, speedy response, and full of vernacular. Of the current crop of characters, I'd most like to meet Lilian. In a gin bar.

The Archers **is wonderful because...** like the motto on early pound coins, it's *semper fidelis* – always loyal. You can not listen for weeks – for months – and drop back in, and Nothing Has Changed. Though thanks to the omnibus podcast, I never do that.

If you could make one change to *The Archers* **it would be...** get rid of all that faux talk about branding – the Tom Archer brand, the Ambridge Organics brand, the Hassett Hills Lamb brand. As if! They flit from being yokels to being multi-channel marketing geniuses.

Sam Knowles, brand storyteller

VILLAGE PRODUCTIONS (ACT I)

Ambridge may not be the East End of London or a particularly dangerous terraced street in Manchester, but it still has its fair share of drama. Of course, nowhere do the villagers revel in the delights of dramatic expression as much as in the amateur productions put on in the Village Hall. Here are details of just some of these theatrical memories.

- **1991 *Aladdin* and *Aladdin*** – Lynda Snell's script for *Aladdin*, which she had staged in Sunningdale a few years before arriving in Ambridge, was rejected by the Village Hall Committee in favour of Bert Fry's for being outdated. Disheartened but not defeated, Lynda decided to go ahead with her own version on the same night at Ambridge Hall. The two plays went head-to-head with Eddie Grundy playing the role of Wishee Washee in both productions, without the directors' knowledge. He was driven to and fro between scenes without them even knowing.
- **1996 *Cinderella*** – Larry Lovell's production of this fairy-tale classic included Lynda Snell as a resentful Fairy Godmother and Larry himself as Baron Hardup. When Lynda was delayed arriving to one performance, Larry decided to perform both roles by himself. The audience definitely got their money's worth when Lynda showed up and both Fairy Godmothers appeared on stage together.
- **1997 *A Midsummer Night's Dream*** – This open-air production, directed by Lynda Snell, was held in the grounds of Lower Loxley. Lynda put aside her competitive feelings towards fellow thespian Larry Lovell and cast him as Theseus

– his preferred role was Lysander, but Lynda decided he was too old for the part.

- 1999 ***Babes in the Millennium Wood*** – Lynda Snell was particularly hurt when Larry Lovell went out of his way to insult her production in his review of this show in the *Borchester Echo*. The review focused on the smell of pig manure rather than commenting on the actors or the direction. His one compliment was reserved for the costumes, put together by Jill Archer.

- 2000 *Mikado* – The show must go on and this one in particular was a great success; but for a while there it looked unlikely that Lynda Snell's production of this W. S. Gilbert comic opera would make it to performance night. Lynda had to deal with Tom Archer's complicated love life causing cast members to quit and Christine Barford putting her back out at the dress rehearsal. Not to mention the real costume drama when the hire company botched their order and sent them the Felpersham Light Opera Society's costumes for Venetian opera *The Gondoliers* instead.

- 2003 ***The Ambridge Mystery Plays*** – With the arrival of new vicar Alan Franks a decision was made to give the Christmas production more of a religious theme. This was a peripatetic production that took place at St Stephen's Church, the village green and Brookfield Farm. It starred Susan Carter as Mary and Kenton Archer as her Joseph.

MEET THE CHARACTERS: CAROL TREGORRAN

Villagers with long memories were delighted to see Carol back in Ambridge in 2014, though the circumstances were sad: the funeral of her husband John at St Stephen's. Being back reminded of her old friends, and she made the decision to return. She moved into Jill's cottage, Glebe, which had been lying empty since Jill went to live with David and Ruth.

Carol originally came to Ambridge in 1954 and set up a market garden there. She was rather ahead of her time, a stylish and independent businesswoman. She married local landowner Charles Grenville in 1961, and they had a son, Richard. But Charles died in 1965. Carol married bookseller John Tregorran two years later, and they had a daughter. After some turbulent times, the couple moved to Bristol in 1990. They returned occasionally for major events such as Phil's funeral.

Following her permanent return, Carol renewed her friendships with Jill and Peggy, and became known for her herbal remedies which she offered at any opportunity. She successfully evaded gossip from Susan and others regarding the possible affair, long ago, between John and Jennifer Aldridge. Carol hinted several times that her marriage had not been a happy one, and Jennifer got it into her head that Carol had perhaps poisoned John; her amateur detective work produced no results, however.

DID YOU KNOW?

- Carol's birth parents were unmarried artists, who separated when Carol was two. Her adoptive parents were killed in the Blitz.

- In 1963, Carol's first husband Charles was badly injured in a car crash. Coincidentally, John Tregorran's first wife Janet was killed in the same accident.

- Jill is godmother to Anna-Louise, Carol's daughter, and Carol is godmother to James, Lilian's son.

- Carol went undercover with Jim to a party hosted by Justin Elliott, to try and find out about Damara Capital's plans for the village.

ISSUES IN AMBRIDGE: HOMOPHOBIA

You can't please everyone all of the time, but on the whole Ambridge residents are an amiable bunch. Unlike other serial dramas, which have seen gay characters suffer painful bullying, violence and prejudice, the programme's first gay couple – Adam Macy and Ian Craig – didn't face many problems from most of the village's conservative set. Compared to some heterosexual relationships and affairs in Ambridge which have caused no end of debate and controversy, Adam and Ian, who shared their first kiss in a strawberry field in April 2004, have had rather less to deal with, other than Sid Perks's homophobia, Ian's coming out to his conservative Protestant family, Adam's stepfather Brian Aldridge's objections to the civil partnership, and Adam's grandmother Peggy feeling uncomfortable about their relationship. Sid, in fact, had previous form with regard to homophobia: he was hostile to Sean Myerson, a gay man and landlord of the nearby Cat and Fiddle pub, when Sean briefly captained the cricket team.

Adam and Ian made history when they had Ambridge's first civil partnership ceremony in 2006 – a year after the UK's first civil partnerships. The episode attracted an extra 250,000 listeners to the programme and was praised by the gay media for its rounded and thoughtful portrayal of a homosexual relationship. The episode made history by being the first serial drama to feature a gay civil ceremony. With the legalisation of same-sex marriage in 2014, Adam and Ian decided to get engaged.

FAMOUS FACES IN AMBRIDGE: PART 4

Thanks to Lynda Snell, Ambridge gets its fair share of culturally important visitors.

★ In 2009, Turner Prize-winning sculptor **Anthony Gormley's** Trafalgar Square project 'One & Other' invited members of the public to apply to stand on a plinth for one-hour time slots over 100 days. After all the Ambridge residents' applications were rejected, Phil suggested Lynda create an Ambridge plinth for the village fête. Gormley was invited to Ambridge to open the fête and judge the participants – a photographic book of his sculptures was the prize for the winner, Molly Button.

★ Lynda Snell's Whodunnit? theme for the 2010 village fête set fans' tongues wagging about which famous mystery writer would be invited to Ambridge to open the event. Fittingly,

Archers fan **Colin Dexter** was chosen and presented the prize for solving the murder mystery. *Archers* editor Vanessa Whitburn saw inviting the author as a great chance to repay the favour for his character Inspector Morse's dedication to *The Archers* in his books.

★ No recent celebrity appearance on the programme has been more talked about than that of the self-confessed '*Archers* addict', **Camilla, Duchess of Cornwall** in 2011. Recorded at Clarence House to mark the 25th anniversary of the National Osteoporosis Society and the sixtieth anniversary of *The Archers*, the Duchess played herself. Her scene mainly consisted of a chat with Caroline and Ian about his 'delicious' homemade shortbread, avoiding any further mention of Prince Charles' rival Duchy Originals biscuits (Ian had previously expressed concern about possible comparisons). Lynda had been looking forward to the visit more than anyone, and was initially disappointed not to meet the Duchess, but later received a 'charming wave and smile' which made up for it.

★ Celebrity cameos were plentiful in 2014. **Sir Bradley Wiggins** kicked things off by presenting the prizes at the Rough and Tumble event in aid of Sport Relief. He handled things calmly, even when Ian punched Rob right in front of him. 'Stand back, fella,' Sir Bradley said, taking the heat out of the situation. After Wiggo, it was **Kirstie Allsopp**'s turn to lend a touch of glamour to Ambridge. She opened the village fête, and took time out to encourage Fallon in her upcycling of old furniture. Barely a month later, in August, the **Pet Shop Boys** stepped in at the last minute as a headline act for the Loxfest music extravaganza, replacing the 'troubled' and perhaps slightly less well-known Quaintance Smith. It was also in 2014 that **Morrissey** revealed that he'd been invited to take a cameo role, but sadly this splendid event has yet to come to pass.

GONE BUT NOT FORGOTTEN:
JACK WOOLLEY

Born: 19 July 1919
Died: 2 January 2014
Played by: Arnold Peters

A pillar of the community for more than fifty years, Jack will be remembered as an entrepreneur and a loving husband. He was probably the most successful businessman Ambridge has ever seen. His long career began with the purchase of Grey Gables Hotel and Country Park, and his portfolio later expanded to include the village shop, Arkwright Hall, the shoot, the controversial Glebelands housing estate and Jaxx Caff. It wasn't all plain sailing though – Jack was unlucky enough to be involved in two robberies. The first, in 1973, took place at Grey Gables, and Jack was left unconscious. The second, twenty years later, was the Horrobin-organised armed raid on the village shop. Jack was hospitalised after this and suffered from panic attacks for some time after.

Jack's first wife died in the 1950s, and he married Valerie Trentham in 1965, a couple of years after he first moved to Ambridge. He legally adopted Valerie's daughter Hazel, but Valerie was unfaithful and the marriage was unhappy. Peggy Archer became his assistant at Grey Gables and he asked her to marry him in the 1970s, but she refused. It wasn't until 1991 that she at last said yes, making him Peggy's second husband called Jack (her first, the troubled Jack Archer, died of liver failure after battling a drink problem). Although Jack's beloved bull terrier, Captain, died while they were on honeymoon, this unlucky start did not prevent Jack and Peggy from enjoying a very happy marriage. It was a sad day when the smart Jack began to lose his memory, gradually succumbing to

Alzheimer's disease. His decline was slow and painful, and finally Peggy could no longer look after him at home and made the difficult decision to put him into care at the Laurels. He passed peacefully away in the first days of 2014. He was always a staunch supporter of the difficult Hazel, but after his death she clashed with Peggy over the will, and the wording on Jack's headstone.

WELCOME TO AMBRIDGE:
THE DOWER HOUSE

- ✷ This fine country house with slate roof and large garden was the residence of Berrow Estate owners Ralph and Lilian Bellamy between 1970 and 1975.

- ✷ The egregious Cameron Fraser lived here in the 1990s and renovated in a flashy style, which didn't go down well with future residents Guy and Caroline Pemberton.

- ✷ Will Grundy lived in the Dower House's self-contained flat after his family were evicted from Grange Farm in 1999.

✼ Self-made businessman Matt Crawford moved into The Dower House with its former mistress, Lilian Bellamy. It was the base for their joint business venture, Amside Property Developments, until Matt scarpered to Costa Rica in 2015, leaving Lilian behind, but taking most of the contents of their house and joint accounts with him.

✼ The Dower House was the temporary refuge for Robert and Lynda Snell during the flood aftermath

OH, SO QUIET!

While some Ambridge folk never know when to keep their mouths shut, others are a little less upfront. *The Archers* gives listeners a glimpse of the different goings-on in the village but never lets us hear everyone or everything, meaning some characters, while being referred to and acknowledged for years on the programme, might never find their voice on the airwaves. Here are some of Ambridge's most silent residents.

✼ **Baggy** – Eddie Grundy's friend helped him create a corn circle, lived on Grange farm with his partner Sylvia (a pagan) and six children in a bus and a tepee, and played the rear end of a cow in the 1998 village production of *Jack and the Beanstalk*..

✼ **Fat Paul** – Another of Eddie Grundy's friends, Fat Paul is heavily tattooed and once put Eddie in touch with loan shark

Mike Butcher. Eddie persuaded him to join in the tug-of-war fundraiser for the pub team in 2004, as a counterweight to Ronnie the farrier on the church's team, but despite his size he wasn't a great help and the pub lost.

- **Mandy Beesborough** – This red-headed gal ran the pony club in 1987 and caught Brian Aldridge's attention – he even invited her to join his party at the horse races on the day his daughter Alice was being born. There was an awkward moment or two when Jennifer's book group decided to read *Mistress of the Paddock* by local author Carinthia Hart, supposedly a thinly-disguised account of Mandy and Brian's alleged dalliance. Some village voices say that nowadays the glorious red of Mandy's hair comes (whisper it) *from a bottle…*

- **Reg Hebden** – Mark and Joanna's father passed away in 2013. He was a solicitor until he retired. He was married to Bunty (who pre-deceased him), and together they insisted their grandson Daniel didn't go to state school.

- **Neville Booth** – Enthusiastic bell-ringer Neville joined the St Stephen's team in 1998 but his car was stolen while he was at practice. He has a nephew called Nathan (also a man of very few words).

- **Derek Fletcher** – Married to Pat, chatty Derek moved into Glebelands in 1983 and visited Meyruelle in France as part of the village-twinning process. He often complains about backache and has a collection of garden gnomes in his garden.

- **Pru Forrest** – Originally voiced by Mary Dalley, the Bull barmaid who married Tom Forrest disappeared into silent-ville in the 1970s and 1980s, despite being involved in a number of important storylines. She worked as a housekeeper at Brookfield Farm and became a determined entrant in the annual Flower and Produce Show. She famously spoke up (played by Judi Dench) and gave the welcoming speech to Terry Wogan when he came to Ambridge in 1989, briefly losing her composure upon first meeting Terry. Pru lived out her last years in The Laurels, and finally took her silent voice to join the heavenly choir in November 1998.

✿ **Freda Fry** – Freda, Bert's wife, passed away in 2015. For a silent character, she was unusually present, and will be greatly missed by listeners. No one will miss her as much as Bert, of course, whose grief was touching – 'the best wife a man could ever have!' They were one of Ambridge's strongest and most loving couples, and Freda was almost certainly the biggest fan of Bert's poetic oeuvre. Freda was famed for her cooking; her pies in particular were a local speciality at The Bull. She spent lots of her time in her own kitchen preparing jams and pickles for the Flower and Produce Show, and presumably listening to Bert declaim his poetry.

✿ **John Higgs** – Formerly Jack Woolley's chauffeur and handyman, Higgs is a keen gardener and long-term smoker who came to Grey Gables in 1966.

✿ **Trudy Porter** – Faithful Trudy first appeared in 1984 working as a waitress at Grey Gables, and slowly rose through the ranks, becoming an assistant manager and receptionist. She once had thespian aspirations and auditioned for a part in one of Lynda Snell's plays. After over thirty years of service she handed in her resignation, speaking for the first time as she did so.

✿ **Eileen Titcombe (previously Pugsley)** – Mrs Titcombe (widow of the late Mr Pugsley) is the housekeeper at Lower Loxley Hall. Her first name wasn't revealed until she married Edgar Titcombe in 2010.

✂ **Edgar Titcombe** – Known by everyone as Titcombe, Lower Loxley's head gardener has always gone above and beyond his job description, taking care of the Pargetters' peacocks, and developing nature trails and a treetop walk in the grounds. He is now married to housekeeper Eileen.

✂ **Bob Pullen** – Other than his regular bladder complaints, this Manorfield Close resident will be remembered for narrowly escaping death when Eddie hurled an axe in his direction at the 1999 village fête. He sadly failed to escape death in December 2012. He left behind a series of rhyming clues for Joe and Bert, which led them to his will, in which he left Joe his lucky keyring.

✂ **Richard and Sabrina Thwaite** – Part of the fashionable and respectable Grange Spinney set, Sabrina's attractive appearance is often crudely referred to by the laddish Ambridge men. She played the cat in the 2010 production of *Dick Whittington*, in which she was heard mewing with a great deal of emotion – a rare treat for *Archers* listeners. Her husband, Richard, is an accountant.

✂ **Lady Mercedes Goodman** – Wife of the late Sir Sidney Goodman, this Spanish señorita is in mourning for her husband who was knighted for his services to industry – he worked in the food-canning business. She enjoys shooting and indulging in some health club pampering. She attended Jack Woolley's funeral, though sadly for the listeners, in silence.

✂ Other current silent characters include: Lower Loxley's resident falconer, **Jessica**; the **Buttons**; assistant herd managers at Berrow Farm, **Becky** and **Raf**; **Barry** from Penny Hassett, whose greatest joy is bursting crisp packets in The Bull; Coriander Snell's partner **Justin Bamford**; **Rosie Mabbott**, Clarrie's younger sister who lives in Great Yarmouth; and Eddie Grundy's old pal **Snatch Foster**.

• QUIZ NIGHT AT THE BULL •

COMPETITIONS, CURTSEYS AND CURTAIN-UPS

1. What event took place instead of the Flower and Produce Show in 1989?

2. In 2008 Lynda Snell attempted to outdo a production of which play put on by Larry Lovell ten years previously?

3. Which Borchester pub renamed itself The Old Corn Mill?

4. Who donated the pig for the barbeque held on the day of Prince Charles and Lady Diana Spencer's wedding?

5. Susan Carter wore the 1998's Easter Bonnet Competition winning bonnet, but who had made the hat?

6. What song helped the Ambridge WI reach the regional finals of a choral competition in 1969?

7. Who was awarded the prize for Longest Runner Bean in the Children's Section at the 1999 Flower and Produce Show?

8. What did Kenton Archer spill on one of Lower Loxley's antique silk carpets during his game of 'Murder'?

9. Which couple donated three ballroom dancing lessons to a 2004 auction to raise money for homeless people in Colombia?

10. Alice Aldridge played the part of Snow White in the 2006 Christmas production, but who played her prince?

11. Who played Scrooge in Lynda Snell's production of *A Christmas Carol*?

12. What part did Susan Carter play in *Blithe Spirit*?

MEMORABLE MOMENTS:
SID AND JOLENE
IN THE SHOWER

Date: 27 January 2000
Location: Jolene's bathroom

As with the assassination of JFK, everyone can remember where they were when they heard Sid and Jolene in the shower. It scarred a generation. The pair had been having an affair for a couple of months when their epic tryst took place. Contrary to popular memory, however, there were no actual shenanigans in the shower – they had apparently taken place earlier, off mic. In fact listening to the scene again (available on the BBC website), we note less the steaminess, which is confined to Jolene lasciviously admiring Sid's 'lovely muscly back', and more the panic that Sid gets into when he realises that Jolene has washed said back with flowery-smelling shower gel. He knows that Kathy will notice the unusual scent, and gets in a lather (sorry); Jolene calms him down by saying that she will use plain coal tar soap instead. And er, that's it. Despite the lack of anything explicit, the British media went into a tailspin. 'Will *The Archers* ever be the same again?' lamented *The Independent*, and *The Scotsman* complained that there had been no nudity warning. It's hard to understand now why we were all so utterly shocked. Maybe it was simply because we had never heard its like on *The Archers* before. There was something ground-breaking about the thought of a middle-aged couple on a cosy show being so racy, and it was clearly a thought that many of us wished we hadn't had.

RIP

GONE BUT NOT FORGOTTEN:
BETTY TUCKER

Born: 4 August 1950
Died: 16 December 2005
Played by: Pamela Craig

Farming may have been in her blood, but loyalty and an inherent goodness were in her heart. Betty Tucker arrived in Ambridge in 1974 newly-wed to Mike and stuck with him until her untimely death in 2005, at only 55 years old. But Mike didn't make those years easy on her by any means, and often it was Betty's resourcefulness, determination and thick skin that kept her family above water. One of Ambridge's more nomadic families, the Tuckers found themselves transplanted from Rickyard Cottage on Brookfield Farm to Willow Farm, where Betty offered bed and breakfast, and then on to the slightly dilapidated Ambridge Farm in 1982. This period saw Betty breeding bees, goats and pedigree sheepdogs before embarking on having babies. After going off the contraceptive pill without Mike's knowledge she fell pregnant with their son Roy, born in 1978, and then gave birth to Brenda in 1981. Two young children, a stressed husband and burgeoning financial difficulties were a lot for Betty to handle, but when Mike was declared bankrupt and their future looked uncertain, she pulled up her bootstraps and accepted a cleaning job for Jennifer Aldridge, cottage thrown in.

Life continued to throw rocks at Betty – she dealt with unwanted advances from employer Brian Aldridge and Mike lost an eye in an accident and sank into depression. She became the main breadwinner when Jack Woolley offered her a job in the village shop, and worked hard despite her husband's protestations.

Eventually she found herself back at Willow Farm after Matthew Thorogood accepted their low offer, funded by the compensation money from Mike's accident. Later life brought some more tragedy – Betty was held hostage in the shop during Clive Horrobin's raid – and thankfully some joy with the marriage of her son Roy to Hayley Jordan and also the birth of his daughter Phoebe (with Kate Madikane), her first grandchild. Betty suffered a heart attack in December 2005. Less than a week later, a second one claimed her life and she was found dead by her life partner, in good times and more importantly in bad, Mike Tucker.

LISTENER PORTRAIT

When and why did you start listening? My mum has always listened to it – if I ring up near 7 p.m. she can't get off the phone quick enough! I just started listening at home, in the car, and on holiday in Wales where we didn't have TV. I remember William being born, which makes me feel very old. When I moved to Mexico to teach English, my mum used to send me packets of PG Tips and tapes of *The Archers*. I played episodes to my students as a listening comprehension. They couldn't tell the difference between a yokel and posh accent, or between most of the characters really. A few years later I got another job on the Pacific coast of Mexico, where I had an office to myself with a computer. I was very excited to find I could listen to

The Archers on the iPlayer. It was pretty bizarre to be listening to it with the jungle outside my window – one day an iguana even ran in when I was listening! I listened to omnibus editions when training for the marathon, and I even love *The Archers* theme music and would choose it as a Desert Island Disc.

Which character would you most like to meet? I'd like to meet Fallon – I'm currently collecting vintage crockery and upcycling furniture like her, and we could talk business plans. Or Bert – we could compare dreadful poetry.

Which character drives you crazy? Susan. I especially hate the way she says 'Jenneefur'. Both Pip and Tom Archer were also intensely irritating – but haven't featured so much recently, and have also both turned into different actors!

If you could make one change to *The Archers* it would be... no sex scenes – any kind of squelchy kissing is so cringeworthy. I especially remember shuddering about Sid and Jolene in the shower.

Jessica Barrah, writer and illustrator

WELCOME TO AMBRIDGE: THE STABLES

- Situated opposite Bull Farm House, The Stables has been home to Shula Hebden Lloyd since 2001 when she moved in with husband Alistair and son Daniel.
- The buildings stand on what was originally known as Sixpenny Farm and then Barratt's farm before being sold to Laura Archer in 1965.
- The Stables is also a full-time livery business for Shula and includes a riding school and indoor riding arena. It also houses Alistair's veterinary practice, though this was rendered unusable by the floods in 2015 and Alistair had to find new temporary premises.
- The property's previous name was Onemomona, a Maori word meaning 'home, sweet home', named by Laura Archer in recognition of her New Zealand connections.

MEET THE CHARACTERS:
THE GRUNDYS

It was typical of the Grundy rotten luck that, when they were flooded out of their cottage, Eddie realised he hadn't paid his insurance premiums. Always just one step from a financial crisis, Clarrie is perpetually exasperated at Eddie's dodgy money-making schemes that rarely come to fruition. Nonetheless, Eddie and Clarrie have a loving marriage and a strong sense of familial duty. The way they look after Eddie's father Joe would put many more respectable families to shame. Relations between sons Will and Ed have never been what you might describe as cordial, and they reached a new low when Emma left Will for Ed. They didn't improve when Ed shot Will's dog Baz. But there was a hint of something more friendly when Will agreed that Emma and Ed could rent his cottage, No. 1 The Green. Then Will was strongly encouraged by everyone to be Ed's best man at his wedding to the Grundy-marrying Emma. Despite expectations, this went off without a hitch, making Clarrie in particular very happy. She has always been hopeful that her two boys will one day be good friends.

Will met Nic Hanson when he helped get her buggy onto a bus. Despite a brief hiatus in their relationship after Will saw Nic smack his son George, they married on New Year's Day, 2012. They now live at Greenwood Cottage with their daughter Poppy, and Nic's children Jake and Mia. Poppy, born in 2013, is one of the two new female additions to the Grundy family. The other is Ed and Emma's daughter Keira Susan, born in 2011.

DID YOU KNOW?

- In 2002 Joe Grundy treated turkey Bathsheba as a pet, and then treated himself to her for Christmas dinner.
- Clarrie paid for her own engagement ring when Eddie proposed.
- When Joe Grundy's wife Susan died he put her personal things in a tin box and stored them in a hayloft on Grange Farm.
- Clarrie gave birth to Ed while visiting her sister Rosie in Great Yarmouth.
- Eddie and Clarrie took part in a 'wife swap' in 2005 to raise money to restore the Cat and Fiddle. They were originally intended to swap with Bert and Freda Fry but ended up switching with Matt Crawford and Lilian Bellamy.
- Alf Grundy, Eddie's brother, used to steal chocolate from Woolworths as a boy.
- When forty-something Alf came back to Ambridge briefly in 1986, he stole the contents of nephew Will's money box and his brother's car stereo.
- Ed has a sheep-shearing business with Jazzer, called Ambridge Shearers.
- Ed Grundy went missing in May 2006, and a police investigation followed. He eventually showed up in hospital in July after being beaten up while sleeping rough on the streets of Borchester. Little George Grundy is named after George Barford – Will inherited his gun. His paternity as Will's son, not Ed's, was confirmed by DNA testing.

• QUIZ NIGHT AT THE BULL •

O COME, ALL YE FAITHFUL

1. In what year was St Stephen's Church consecrated?

2. Which vicar was instrumental in setting up the football team The Ambridge Wanderers?

3. What was Robin Stokes's other part-time job as well as being a non-stipendiary minister for Ambridge?

4. A vote was held in 1996 to decide the fate of which vicar?

5. Norris Buckland was a controversial vicar who moved to Ambridge for a year in 1955 – where did he come from?

6. Who resigned as church warden over Alan Franks's marriage to Usha Gupta?

7. A memorial window in St Stephens commemorates which Ambridge resident?

8. Name the couple who caused quite a stir in the church when they decided to marry in 1979 because one of them had previously been divorced?

9. In which country did the Reverend Jerry Buckle serve as a lieutenant in the Grenadier Guards?

10. In 1990 what crashed to the floor of the church narrowly missing Will Grundy?

11. Which rough sleeper did Alan Franks give a sleeping bag to?

12. In addition to Ambridge, Alan looks after three other local parishes. Which are they?

FACT FILE:
CURRENT CAST MEMBERS

Phillip Molloy (Will Grundy) is the real-life son of **Terry Molloy** (Mike Tucker) and Heather Barrett, who voiced vicar's wife Dorothy Adamson in the 1970s and 1980s. And **William Troughton** (Tom Archer) is the real-life son of his Ambridge dad, **David Troughton** (Tony Archer)!

Continuing the theme of well-known relations, **Angus Imrie**, the voice of Josh Archer, is the son of actress Celia Imrie.

Susie Riddell, who plays Tracy Horrobin, had an earlier stint on the programme in the early nineties, playing a young Kate Aldridge. She took that role when she was just eleven years old.

Tasmanian-born **Timothy Bentinck** (David Archer) once took some time off working on *The Archers* to help his own father renovate a small farm in Devon – he even helped deliver twin lambs during a snowstorm.

William Gaminara, who voices Richard Locke (and played him in the 1990s too), also took the part of Johan, a university teacher in Johannesburg who had an affair with Kate Madikane in *Ambridge Extra*. William may be best known for his role as Professor Leo Dalton in *Silent Witness*.

Charles Collingwood and **Judy Bennett** (Brian Aldridge and Shula Hebden Lloyd) married in real life after recording three children's puppet TV shows together. Their off-air relationship has survived Brian's numerous on-air liaisons!

In the 1980s **Alison Dowling** (Elizabeth Pargetter) was also known for her roles in two other serial dramas – *Crossroads* and *Emmerdale*.

Former prime minister Clement Atlee was the grandfather of **Richard Atlee** (Kenton Archer).

Ryan Kelly (Jazzer) has been blind from birth. He is the only cast member on *The Archers* to learn his lines for recording, rather than read them from a script.

In 2000 **Patricia Gallimore** (Pat Archer) published a book titled *Patricia Gallimore's Organic Year: A Guide to Organic Living*.

When **Patricia Greene** (Jill Archer) joined the programme in 1956 she was so inexperienced in radio acting techniques that when the script called for Jill to pour a cup of coffee over Phil Archer, the actress drenched Norman Painting with a cup of water.

When **Charlotte Martin's** character Susan Carter was put in prison for harbouring her fugitive brother in 1993, the actress was asked to appear on talk show *Kilroy* to discuss women prisoners, but turned down the opportunity because she thought it would blur the line between fact and fiction.

Felicity Finch, who plays Ruth, is also a features and documentary presenter for Radio 4, can regularly be heard on *Woman's Hour*, and has worked in broadcasting in Afghanistan.

In the 1960s **Angela Piper** (Jennifer Aldridge) used to read the letters for the BBC's *Points of View* programme.

Brian Hewlett, who plays Neil, says one of the favourite roles he has played is Tevye in *Fiddler on the Roof*.

Teacher **Lesley Saweard** took over the role of Christine Barford after Pamela Mant left the show in the 1950s. She was asked to audition after a chance meeting with Denis Folwell (Jack Archer) when he commented on the similarity of the two actresses' voices.

June Spencer (Peggy Woolley) played both Peggy and Irish lass Rita Flynne in 1951. She took a break from both roles to adopt two children in 1953, and while she returned sporadically a year later to voice the smaller part of Rita, she wouldn't voice Peggy again until 1962.

Graham Blockey, who plays Robert, is married to Christine Ingram, best known for her many cookery books. She was a writer for *The Archers* for a short period in the 1990s.

Clarrie Grundy was originally voiced by **Heather Bell.** The role was taken over by Rosalind Adams in 1988, but when she left in 2013, Heather Bell returned.

WELCOME TO AMBRIDGE: THE VICARAGE

- This four-bedroom bungalow was built in 1974 on the site of the old Georgian Vicarage building.
- When Robin Stokes left Ambridge for a new job in Surrey in 1995 he would leave the Vicarage bereft of a vicar until Reverend Alan Franks moved in in 2003. He had lived briefly at the Darrington Vicarage, but it was found to have structural defects.
- 1997 saw Dr Richard Locke convert the Vicarage into his surgery practice.
- Before it was the village surgery the Church authorities used the Vicarage as a holiday home for underprivileged children.
- Now Reverend Alan Franks lives there with his wife Usha; their living room is decorated with a statue of Hindu deity Shiva.

LISTENER PORTRAIT

When and why did you start listening? Because my father listened every day, twice a day and to the omnibus edition, from the very beginning.

What's your most memorable Ambridge moment? The death of Grace Archer in the burning barn.

Which character would you most like to meet? Rob, because he's so vile.

Which character drives you crazy? Ruth.

***The Archers* is wonderful because…** it passes the time while I'm getting supper.

Josephine Trotter, painter

GONE BUT NOT FORGOTTEN:
WALTER GABRIEL

Born: 25 August 1896
Died: 3 November 1988
Played by: Chris Gittins

The large Gabriel family were traditionally the blacksmiths of Ambridge, but Walter went against the grain and was working as a tenant farmer of the Squire in 1951. He bought and sold his farm on, moving to Honeysuckle Cottage. Considered by many to be an inept farmer – neighbour Dan Archer was constantly complaining about his broken fences and dilapidated buildings – Walter was a popular, sociable member of the community whose true vocation was propping up the bar at The Bull. He regularly participated in the Flower and Produce Show and contributed to the village fête.

Having lost his wife Annie at a young age, he invested much of his energy into his son Nelson, whom he greatly admired. In Walter's eyes Nelson could do no wrong. Even when Nelson faked his own death to avoid being prosecuted for the Borchester mail van robbery Walter still insisted on his innocence and took his son on a cruise after his acquittal. Nelson's clearly inherited his entrepreneurial spirit from his father, who dabbled in a pet shop, junk shops, a craft studio and a caravan site in his time. Walter provided comic relief for his Ambridge friends and they showed their gratitude when at his 92nd birthday party he was declared a freeman of The Bull, with Sid Perks announcing all his special ales would be on the house. Despite his determination to go on forever and make the most of Sid's generosity, less than three months later he died of pneumonia.

QUIZ NIGHT AT THE BULL

DOWN ON THE FARM

1. Which farm is responsible for running the Ambridge Organics farm shop?

2. What kind of beef is sold online by David and Ruth Archer?

3. Who sold their herd of Guernsey cows in 2015?

4. How many acres was Brookfield Farm when Dan Archer bought it in 1954?

5. Which of Ambridge's farms is the largest with 1,585 arable acres?

6. Which of the following is not a name of one of the fields at Bridge Farm: Queencups, Primrose Bank or Big Leys?

7. Which business at Willow Farm did Josh Grundy buy a partnership in?

8. Which family were forced out of Grange Farm due to bankruptcy in 2000?

9. Home farm is home to a maze, but what's it made from?

10. In what year did Dan Archer lose most of his oats when a fire broke out in his Dutch barn?

11. What's the name of the 'mega-dairy' in Ambridge?

12. Where did Pip Archer meet Spencer Wilkes?

MAKING THE ARCHERS:
SOUNDS LIKE...

Some *Archers* fans are convinced Ambridge is a real place, made up of real houses, a real pub and real barns, stables and vehicles, and it's not hard to hear why. The production of sound effects and sound mixing involves a mixture of sophisticated technology and everyday objects to make listeners believe their favourite characters are really rehearsing a pantomime at the village hall, sipping a pint at The Bull or simply relaxing in their kitchen. The show is recorded at the BBC's Birmingham premises at the Mailbox complex in a state-of-the-art studio space. Different areas of the studio produce a variety of acoustics to recreate the aural feel of a small room, a large hall or a pub. There's even a kitchen with all the modern appliances Ambridge families use. There are two different sinks for washing-up type effects: a smart ceramic Belfast sink, for the more well-heeled characters such as Jennifer, and a stainless steel B&Q one for the Grundys. Sharp-eared *Archers* listeners can apparently tell the difference! Similarly, there is an Aga range and a Comet cooker – although these aren't used for cooking, the doors being opened and closed seemingly sound quite distinct. If the characters are required to eat during a scene, they really do have food, though not usually the item they're meant to be eating. Bananas are used quite regularly, as they don't require much chewing.

The characters in *The Archers* don't spend all their time indoors, so the sound effects artists have a number of clever ways of creating the sounds you'd expect to hear, despite being inside a studio. Actors tread on scrunched up old rolls of tape to record the sound of walking on grass, an old metal ironing board opening and closing stands in for animal pen gates, and an Alka-Seltzer dissolving in a glass of water is often used for the sound of champagne bubbles. The ironing board is very versatile, as it is also used for the sound of putting cumbersome things into the backs of trucks, and for cattle grids. Charles Collingwood (Brian Aldridge) is quoted as saying, 'If the studio ever caught fire, the first thing I'd save would be that ironing board.'

The younger cast members, such as the actors who play George, Keira and Henry, are recorded separately, though the noise of a squeaky-wheeled buggy being pushed is created by a real buggy.

Luckily for *The Archers* cast, radio means they don't really have to punch each other in the face – they have vegetables for that. If you get kicked by a cow, as Brian Aldridge once was, you won't have to come face to face with any crazed bovines. Why bother, when a log striking a cabbage creates a perfectly suitable sound? Some things in life, however, are far more pleasant. Actors on the show used to kiss their hands when the script called for a smooch between two characters, and it wasn't until 1979, after 28 years of hand-kissing, that Nick Wearing and Shula Archer's actors Gareth Johnson and Judy Bennett shared the first real *Archers* kiss. (It was the introduction of stereo recording that made the hand-kissing effects unworkable, as the sound had to come from only one direction, close to the voices!) And if kissing leads on to anything else, there's a bed in the studio for pillow-talk scenes because, according to scriptwriter Keri Davies, 'Your voice sounds different when you are lying down.'

MEET THE CHARACTERS: DR RICHARD LOCKE

Listeners who wonder why Shula and Usha have a frosty relationship need look no further than GP Richard Locke, who reappeared in 2015 after a 17-year absence. Back in the late nineties, Richard was living happily with Usha when Shula and he became close, while he was helping treat Daniel, then a toddler, who was suffering from juvenile arthritis. Shula and Richard's affair caused the end of his relationship with Usha, and created a breach between Shula and Alistair, who had been together for less than a year. With all their lives in disarray, Richard fled to Manchester.

Now Richard's back, working in a GP practice in Felpersham, and delighted to reconnect with Shula and other old friends.

DID YOU KNOW?

- Before Richard left Ambridge, he tried to collect some of his furniture, but Usha had already given it away to charity.
- Richard had been married to a woman called Chloe during his years away from Ambridge, but it didn't work out and he returned to the area as a divorcé.
- Richard sounds rather like Alan, which suggests that Usha has a penchant for men with a Yorkshire accent.

WELCOME TO AMBRIDGE: VILLAGE HALL

- The Village Hall was once the village's own school but has been the home for the playgroup, the WI, the Over Sixties Club, the Flower and Produce Show and many of Lynda Snell's ambitious theatrical productions.
- The Hall had a facelift in 1976 after an electrical fire caused damage to the kitchen extension, and then a complete refurbishment in 1993 with the help of celebrity project coordinator Anneka Rice.
- In 2000 new toilets known as the Jubilee Loos were installed at the Hall after a successful grant application and local fundraising.
- Tony Archer and Eddie Grundy held their joint 50th birthday celebrations at the Hall in 2009.
- Manorfield Close is a cul-de-sac of twelve 'old people's' bungalows opposite the Village Hall. Residents have included Mrs Potter, Mrs Perkins and Colonel Danby.

ISSUES IN AMBRIDGE:
RACISM

It would be wrong to call Ambridge a multi-cultural village, but the introduction of a few out-of-towners of different races and religions has given writers the opportunity to explore issues of racism and prejudice. Usha Gupta (now Franks) – a Ugandan-born Asian solicitor (by way of Coventry) – was the first character to experience the prejudice of some country folk when she was the victim of racist attacks in 1995. She was mugged, had a rock thrown at the window of her cottage and racist slogans and a swastika painted on the walls. Usha almost left Ambridge for good after thugs threw ammonia in her face, leaving her with a corneal abrasion and fear of losing her sight.

Kate Aldridge's father, Brian, revealed more of his own prejudices when his daughter's South African boyfriend Lucas Madikane arrived in Ambridge. Perhaps surprisingly in conservative-minded Ambridge, despite the pair's mixed-race, illegitimate child, the community was very accepting of the polite, educated, charming newcomer and the writers chose not to focus much on Lucas's race, even though he was the first black male character to appear on the programme.

Despite being part of the community since the early 1990s, Hindu Usha faced more problems when she planned to marry the Reverend Alan Franks. The union was a real cause for concern, especially amongst the more stalwart Christians in the village. Shula Hebden Lloyd even went so far as to make disparaging comments in the *Borchester Echo* about the couple's relationship, which led to her resignation as church warden. While church life may not play a huge part in the lives on Ambridge's youth, the parish still fulfils a vital role in the village and for the more religiously fervent members of the community, its presence is paramount.

More recently, Jazzer accused Lynda of racism against the Scots when she tried to quash his idea of a Highland Games, but he swiftly recanted.

LISTENER PORTRAIT

When and why did you start listening? No one ever listened to *The Archers* in my family until my daughter started when she was about 11. I'm afraid I was initially rather scornful. The main radio was in the kitchen and she would listen while eating her supper. Then because my wife was in the kitchen she started listening too, and she got hooked. I came along two or three years after they started. My daughter hasn't listened to it for a long time, but my son took over and is still passionate about it. The big story when I started taking notice was Brian breaking it to everyone that Siobhan's kid was his.

What's your most memorable Ambridge moment? Probably the gay kiss (Adam and Ian). A friend of mine, a gay man and avid *Archers* fan, read in the paper that it was due to happen and there was great excitement.

Which character would you most like to meet? For very different reasons my favourite characters used to be Matt and Usha, but Matt's gone, sadly, and presumably won't be returning, and something's gone wrong with Usha's character since she married Alan. I do like Adam, I always agree with him when he gets exasperated with Brian and Debbie. He seems a decent guy.

Which character drives you crazy? This is very difficult, as there are so many to choose from. It used to be Kathy and Shula, but it seems Dan sharing Shula's genes is going to surpass his mother in sheer horror. I also loathe Peggy and Jill but I wouldn't want them to know that – I feel guilty about saying it because they're getting on a bit.

If you could make one change to *The Archers* it would be... a better class of gossip. It's usually so basic – Susan in the village shop. What we need and what we expect is more malicious gossip. For instance, Ed and Emma getting together after she split with Will is extraordinary, but no one ever mentions it or even raises an eyebrow. In real life it would have been the talk of the village for years. But I only remember Matt mentioning it once, in the pub.

David Jarman, bookseller

NOT FROM ROUND 'ERE

While it's hard to imagine a nicer place to be from than Ambridge, many of the village's residents have been 'incomers', moving to the small Borsetshire haven from all over the globe. Here are just some of the former habitats of Ambridge dwellers.

Majorie Antrobus – Burma; Palestine; Rhodesia; Waterley Cross
Laura Archer – South Otago, New Zealand; Stourhampton
Ruth Archer – Prudhoe, Northumberland
George Barford – Yorkshire
Jeremy Buckle – Nairobi; Derbyshire
Ian Craig – Northern Ireland
Matt Crawford – Peckham
Usha Franks – Kampala, Uganda; Coventry
Cameron Fraser – Scotland
Simon Gerrard – Canada
Siobhan Hathaway – Ireland; London
Jethro Larkin – Dorset
Richard Locke – Manchester
Lucas Madikane – Langa, Cape Town
Jazzer McCreary – Glasgow
Jolene Archer – Huddersfield
Polly Perks – East End; Penny Hassett
Sid Perks – Birmingham
Johnny Phillips – Leeds
Ellen Rogers – Spain
Lynda Snell – Sunningdale
Oliver Sterling – North Borsetshire
Matthew Thorogood – Papua New Guinea
Martha Woodford – Penny Hassett
Hazel Woolley – Bahamas
Jack Woolley – Stirchley, Birmingham

QUIZ NIGHT AT THE BULL

AMBRIDGE EXTRA

1. How many series of *Ambridge Extra* have there been?

2. Who fell for Dmitry's charms while in St Petersburg?

3. What keepsake did Bert Fry take from Bob Pullen's house, after Bob died?

4. How did Alice help Chris raise the money to buy out his old boss's business?

5. What dark secret about his first wife, Catherine, did Alan discover from her mother Mabel?

6. Who did Alistair share an illicit kiss with?

7. Who did Amy Franks hit with her car?

8. Which former business partner did Kenton run into while visiting Meriel in New Zealand?

9. Phoebe made a new friend while visiting Kate in South Africa. What was her name?

10. Where were Fallon, Jazzer and Harry heading when their van broke down in Cumbria?

11. Alan was accused of what by Colonel Aubrey Shawcross?

12. What happened to Nicolai Barbarin, a businessman who swindled Matt and his Russian contact Vitaly?

WELCOME TO AMBRIDGE: VILLAGE SHOP

- While many villages have seen the disappearance of their local shop or post office in recent years, Ambridge have held on to theirs with a tight fist – the community rallied together in 2010 to save the shop from closure and it is now largely run by volunteers, led by Susan Carter.
- Following the flood in 2015, the shop was set up temporarily on Bridge Farm.
- Martha Woodford worked as manager and then part-time in the shop, spreading gossip for decades. She also introduced an off-licence section and a home-delivery service during her time there.
- In 1990 Jack Woolley installed a flashing neon sign, which immediately prompted a village-wide campaign for its removal.
- There have been two armed raids on the shop over the years, which must be a higher than average statistic for a peaceful country village.

MEET THE CHARACTERS:
MOLLY AND TILLY BUTTON

Despite not saying much, sisters Molly and Tilly Button are allegedly quite wild spirits. They are very involved in village life, and can be relied upon to turn up to every event, sometimes causing mild chaos. Brown Owl once had to 'have a word' with Tilly, though for what was unclear. Molly tends to win all the Easter bonnet contests and fancy dress competitions, once memorably dressing up as mushroom. Possibly relatedly, Mr Button (who we rarely hear from) has been described as the county fungi expert. The sisters joined forces to present a Thai coconut dance at 'Christmas Round the World'.

Molly once rescued Oliver's fly-away hat; but she blotted her copybook, hat-wise, in 2015 when she and Tilly were prime suspects for pinching the May Queen's crown. Perhaps they were disgruntled that for once, someone else had won something (Mia, in this case).

DID YOU KNOW?

- Molly was very upset when her tap-dance failed to win a prize at the Ambridge Has Talent show.

- Molly is friends with Phoebe.

- Johnny was spotted talking to Molly animatedly on Bonfire Night, but nothing much came of it.

- Molly once pinched Ruari's bottom.

- Molly was Jim's secret informant at the Great Bird Race, telling him the whereabouts of a red kite.
- The first time we ever heard of Tilly Button was at the Single Wicket competition in 2011. She was, perhaps surprisingly given her later behaviour, quietly reading a book.

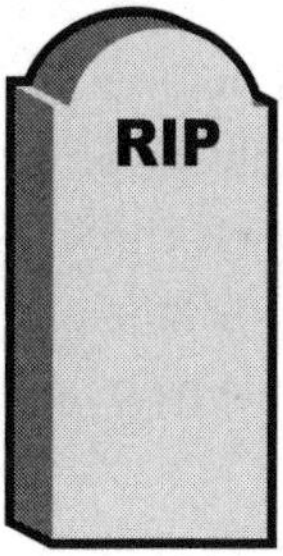

GONE BUT NOT FORGOTTEN:

DANIEL 'DAN' ARCHER

Born: 15 October 1896
Died: 23 April 1986
Played by: Frank Middlemass

The legacy of Dan and his wife Doris can be seen in almost all of the programme's current crop of characters, which has led him to be considered by many to be the father of *The Archers* as we know it. A traditional Borsetshire farmer through and through, Dan came to the profession after a stint in the 16th Battalion of the Borchester Regiment during World War One, after which he returned to his home village of Ambridge and took over the management of Brookfield Farm, previously run by his father, and settled down with Doris. Dan's life would have been considerably different if it weren't for his three children – Jack, Phil and Christine – whose relationships, own families and health problems all added to the drama at Brookfield over the years. With Jack taking up a post as landlord at The Bull, Christine uninterested in running Brookfield and Phil butting heads with his father over modern versus traditional methods, Dan came close to selling up the farm he had worked so hard to buy, believing he would never pass it on to his offspring. Luckily, Phil came around and was able to take over from his father when he retired in 1970.

Through all the ups and downs of life in Ambridge – brother-in-law Tom Forrest's manslaughter trial, the death of son Jack, Christine's unhappy marriage to Paul Johnson and the 1956 foot-and-mouth outbreak that saw all the Brookfield cattle destroyed – one woman was with Dan throughout. His almost 60-year marriage to Doris and who knows how many beef and mushroom pies brought Dan true happiness and comfort – something that was hard for him to live without when Doris died in 1980. The loyal family man struggled on for another six years, immersing himself in the lives of his children and grandchildren, but was never quite the same. Dedicated and hard-working to the last, he died of a heart attack while helping a sheep get back on its feet.

VILLAGE PRODUCTIONS (ACT II)

✂ 2004 *A Christmas Carol* – This Lynda Snell production was overshadowed for some Ambridge residents by a dark cloud in the shape of Owen King. When Kathy Perks suggested the seemingly lonely chef take over the role of Mr Fezziwig after Neville Booth dropped out, she couldn't have imagined it would lead to him raping her in the Village Hall. With Kathy traumatised and scared to leave her house, Lynda took over the role, and when Owen King didn't show up for opening night (because Sid had scared him out of Ambridge) Reverend Alan Franks stepped in and gave the part his best shot, much to Lynda's relief.

✂ **2005** *The Spirit of Christmas* – This year's Christmas production was not so much a play, but a festive revue showcasing the best of Ambridge's performing talents. The show was conceived by Julia Pargetter-Carmichael, who beat Lynda Snell to booking up the Village Hall at Christmas, much to Lynda's chagrin, and then passed away in November, leaving Lynda to step up and bring the show together. Performances included open-mic comedy from Kenton Archer, a dance performance by Izzy Blake and Pip Archer and 'Frosty the Snowman' sung by the village children.

✂ **2006** *Snow White and the Seven (Slightly Taller Than Average) Dwarves* – This production saw Lynda Snell doing what she does best – bossing people around and chastising them for smoking, missing rehearsals and not taking their roles seriously enough. There was even a revolt of the dwarves at one rehearsal and arguments about who was the tallest dwarf. Opening night saw Chris Carter as 'Teeny' plugging Tom Archer's sausages while the local journalists were witness to some high drama at the press performance when Joe Grundy accidentally set his dwarf beard on fire and had to be extinguished by Brian Aldridge.

✂ **2008** *Jack and the Beanstalk* – Oh, poor Lynda! This year was as difficult as any other with numerous cast members being replaced due to illness and lack of commitment and her frustrations of no one learning their lines on time. Despite all the chopping and changing, the opening night was a huge success – even with Mike Tucker's ad-libbing – and in part thanks to Alistair Lloyd's technical effects. Because Eddie Grundy had refused to dance around in the cow costume, Lynda and husband Robert stepped in at the last minute, with Lynda taking the rear-end spot. Unfortunately, during the show her hair got caught up in the costume and she had to be cut free from the cow.

✼ 2010 *The Strange Affair at Ambridge Towers* – In addition to the annual Christmas production, 2010 saw more theatrics than usual when the village fête played host to both celebrity guest Colin Dexter and Lynda's complicated murder mystery play. Cast members included Emma Grundy, Jill Archer and a theatrically-challenged David Archer as the policeman. The prize for solving the mystery was two signed Inspector Morse books, which was won by Vicky and Mike Tucker.

✼ 2010 *Dick Whittington* – Rehearsals for this Christmas panto saw Fallon Rogers and milkman Harry Mason making up their own lines and flirting like schoolchildren, much to the annoyance of a jealous Jack 'Jazzer' McCreary. Lynda put on the production especially for her step-grandson Oscar Snell who was happy to meet the cat (played by Sabrina Thwaite) after the show. Felpersham Light Opera Society director Tristram Hawkshaw attended the opening night and wrote a favourable review for the *Echo*.

✼ 2011 *Christmas Round the World* – This troubled production featured Jazzer singing 'Have Yourself a Merry Little Christmas', one of Elona's daughters playing some Albanian music, and Jim reading from Virgil, among other delights. Lynda was just relieved that Jim read an English translation, rather than the original Latin.

✼ 2012 *Elizabethan Extravanganza* – Kenton led this bawdy night as 'Lord of Misrule', having refused to give Lynda much of a clue as to what he was planning. His jokey asides and the pig's bladder on a stick (actually a balloon), with which he biffed various participants over the head, meant that Lynda went through no end of wincing. But Robert managed to convince her that Kenton wasn't ruining the acts, and in fact was enhancing them. Kenton dedicated the show to the late Bob Pullen, and remembered to thank Lynda, soothing her ruffled feathers.

- 2013 *Robin Hood* – Lynda had been hoping for something a little different this year. With the initial casting of Maurice as a grizzled Robin, and Anthea as his Marian, Lynda envisaged a twilight-years retelling of the famous story. However, the main actors bailed out and she had to make do with Rob (still married to Jess) and Kirsty (not best pleased about her mate Helen being messed about by Rob). The two spent rehearsals glaring at each other angrily, until an embarrassing scene in which Lynda innocently asked Rob to try and recall romantic feelings to enhance his flat performance. He stormed off, and Tom was brought in as a late replacement. His love scenes with Kirsty were so realistic that even Lynda was pleased, and Tom and Kirsty became engaged just before the performance.

- 2014 *Blithe Spirit* – A first for Radio 4, as they broadcast a full production of this play on Boxing Day, with the actors playing their Archers' characters playing Coward's characters. Confusing, but it seemed to work. Rehearsals were as fraught as always, however, with Helen devastated after Tony's accident with the bull, and only returning to her role at the last minute. Lynda was ideal as Madame Arcati, and was thus perhaps justified in her disappointment when the person most praised by local critic Tristram Hawkshaw was Susan Carter, hamming it up as the maid.

QUIZ NIGHT AT THE BULL

EVENTS OF THE YEAR

1. What colour did Pip Archer dye her hair on April Fool's Day to wind up her parents?

2. Whose jawbone was found in the village pond in 1990?

3. In what year did The Bull open a Civil War-themed restaurant?

4. Who led the Ambridge Scout Troop in the 1970s?

5. Which Archer dressed as Superman for the County Hotel's fancy dress ball in 1983?

6. Who scooped a record fifteen first prizes at the 1985 Flower and Produce Show?

7. What was Elizabeth wearing when she came third in the 1986 Penny Hassett pancake race?

8. What did Shula Hebden Lloyd bet Alistair he wouldn't be able to give up for Lent in 2000?

9. Who represented Ambridge's WI at a Buckingham Palace garden party in 1965?

10. Which band was replaced at the last minute by the Pet Shop Boys, at Loxfest?

11. After learning of the existence of Ruairi Donovan, what did Alice throw in the bin on Father's Day?

12. Whose hand was burnt by a firework on Bonfire Night in 1991?

PORTRAIT OF THE WRITER AS A LISTENER:

DAVID AARONOVITCH

David Aaronovitch is a writer, broadcaster and columnist Times *columnist.*

When and why did you start listening? As a child. I was born *Archers*, I did not have them thrust upon me. My mother listened and I picked up the habit from her. One of my earliest memories is lying in bed as a small child with the evening theme tune playing (we were put to bed very early).

What's your most memorable Ambridge moment? I have always 'enjoyed' the moment when the innocent spouse realises that her partner is having an affair. When the penny drops, if you like. Kathy with Sid, Jennifer (several times) with Brian, Matt with Lilian. The exception was the ridiculous and mutual David-and-Ruth adultery story.

Which character would you most like to meet? If I was 25 years younger? Fallon. She's fabulous.

Which character drives you crazy? The usual: Ruth, Pip, the new Tom, Kirsty, Ian (yawn…), Bert. Moaning, platitudinous, two-dimensional, etc.

The Archers **is wonderful because...** it may not be wonderful at all. It's a habit and I have a very clear notion of which friends and relatives I can discuss Ambridge with and which ones think I'm mad.

If you could make one change to *The Archers* **it would be...** to bring back Matt and seed a new adultery storyline in around now.

MEMORABLE MOMENTS:
JENNIFER SMASHING BRIAN'S GIFT OF PERFUME

Date: 7 January 2003
Location: Home Farm

It was Jennifer's birthday, but she wasn't exactly in a party mood. She had learned of Brian's affair with Siobhan Hathaway just three weeks earlier. That she found out was thanks to Debbie, who realised that Siobhan's new baby, Ruairi, bore an extraordinary resemblance to Alice. Plus Debbie saw that when Siobhan mopped up the baby's sick, she did so with one of Brian's monogrammed hankies! Ah, the vanity and folly of the personalised tissue.

Debbie confronted Brian, forced the truth out of the blackguard, and made him tell Jennifer.

For three weeks after this, there was of course much upset, anger, tension and, in Jennifer's case, putting on a brave public face. (And in Brian's case, presenting a bashed public face – he had a black eye courtesy of Tim, Siobhan's husband.) But finally, on Jennifer's birthday, her stiff upper lip trembled. Brian gave her a present – a bottle of perfume – and Jenny stared at in horror, saying that this was the sort of present a man gave his mistress. She then lost it completely, smashing the perfume on the floor , at which we all winced, imagining the choking scent rising up, not to mention the shards of glass. And she screamed, 'Give it to your whore!'

WELL! We'd have choked on our suppers, if they weren't lying cold and untouched, as we listened to the most gripping radio some of us have ever heard, before or since.

After a great deal of soul-searching, Jennifer finally forgave Brian. She even agreed to take Ruairi, offspring of the affair, into their home after Siobhan's death, which seemed rather saintly to us.

WELCOME TO AMBRIDGE: WILLOW FARM

- In 1972 Haydn Evans bought this full working farm for his son Gwyn. The land has since been divided and sold off over time to Phil Archer, Brian Aldridge and Bill Insley.
- The farmhouse is now divided into two properties: Willow Cottage where Mike, Vicky and Bethany Tucker lived until recently, and the adjoining Willow Farm where Roy and Hayley Tucker lived with daughters Phoebe and Abbie, until Roy and Hayley split. Since then, Roy's been living in the farm alone.
- There is a memorial apple tree for Mike's late first wife, Betty, in the garden.
- Eight acres of Willow Farm land are owned by Neil Carter, who has an outdoor herd of breeding sows and an organic free-range egg business.
- Neil Carter, with Mike's help, built wife Susan her dream house – Ambridge View – on his plot of Willow Farm land.

MEET THE CHARACTERS: THE HORROBINS

Was ever a surname more apt? The 'orrible Horrobins have caused untold problems in Ambridge, particularly Clive and brother Keith, who have between them committed armed robbery, arson, assault and intimidation. Mum Ivy did her best with a bad lot, and continued to support Clive and visit him in prison even after he was charged with grievous bodily harm. When Ivy died in 2011, Bert and son Gary struggled to manage on their own, and Bert's daughter Tracy and her kids moved in with them (once she and Susan had 'strongly encouraged' Neil to renovate the place). Of all the Horrobin siblings, it's Susan who has moved the furthest away from her poor start, making a decent marriage and carving out an upstanding village life, so it was a massive shock to all when she was imprisoned briefly for harbouring fugitive Clive.

DID YOU KNOW?

- Three of Bert and Ivy's six children have spent time at Her Majesty's pleasure: Clive, Keith and Susan. Keith's still in there, doing time for arson.
- Clive Horrobin was caught trespassing in the Country Park when he was eleven.
- Pinky, the pig Susan Horrobin won at the village fête in 1983, brought Neil Carter close to Susan – he helped her care for the pig.

- Tracy Horrobin was the bridesmaid at sister Susan's wedding to Neil.

- Clive Horrobin abandoned girlfriend Sharon Richards and his new baby Kylie six weeks after she was born.

- Bert Horrobin enjoys drinking, smoking and playing cards.

GONE BUT NOT FORGOTTEN:
SIOBHAN HATHAWAY
(NÉE DONOVAN)

Born: 13 June 1965   Died: 31 May 2007
Played by: Caroline Lennon

When Siobhan arrived in Ambridge from London in 1999 – the wife of the new village doctor, Tim Hathaway – and fell in love with the quaint countryside village and adorable Honeysuckle Cottage, it's unlikely anyone pigeonholed her as a husband-snatching adulteress. As it turned out, Siobhan ended up being at the centre of one of *The Archers*' most controversial and long-running storylines. A translator by trade, Siobhan struggled to adjust to the gossipy nature of communication adopted by the village, especially when her miscarriage became common knowledge. She soon adjusted to village life, however, and became good friends with Elizabeth Archer. A new job working for a publisher saw her travelling more and more and indirectly encouraged her husband to pursue his feelings for the vicar, Janet Fisher.

The couple's stressful Christmas in 2000 was the setting for Tim's kiss with Janet; he also gave her a scarf he'd previously given to an ungrateful Siobhan who said it wasn't her colour. The dalliance didn't progress after Siobhan confronted him, but it was enough to push her into the arms of Brian Aldridge. After an affair that resulted in Siobhan becoming pregnant, and despite Brian's love for Siobhan, he chose to stay with wife Jennifer. With her own marriage in tatters Siobhan fled to Germany. She reverted to her maiden name, Donovan, and began a relationship with Dieter. Her son Ruairi was born in 2002 and although Brian kept in regular contact, visiting his son secretly on supposed business trips to Hungary, the couple did not reunite. In April 2007, Siobhan revealed to Brian that she was suffering from advanced malignant melanoma and asked him to raise Ruairi if she died. She succumbed to the disease weeks later knowing Ambridge's most controversial baby would return to the village to be with his father.

MAKING THE ARCHERS: FRONT PAGE NEWS

Whether it's celebrity appearances – such as Camilla, Duchess of Cornwall's recent cameo on the show – or anniversary episodes, *The Archers* storylines have been finding their way into the British papers for over 60 years. Dedicated *Archers* fans have become rather attached to the characters in Ambridge, and that attachment is never more obvious than when something truly tragic and terrible happens to the Borsetshire bunch they've come to know and love. The earliest high-profile example of the programme making the news was Grace Archer's death in 1955. The headline-grabbing story, which saw Phil's new wife trapped in a burning barn, aired on the night commercial broadcaster ITV first went on air, and afterwards letters of mourning flooded into the BBC. The story made the front page of some papers and the *Daily Express* demanded 'Why do this to Grace Archer?' The production team decided not to broadcast the funeral as they were concerned too many wreaths would be delivered to the studio. A similar outpouring of grief and shock occurred when Shula's husband Mark Hebden died in a car accident, made even more shocking by *Archers* editor Vanessa Whitburn's own near-fatal car crash a week before Mark's. And even that was overshadowed by Nigel's dramatic roof plunge, which was widely reported in the press, and inspired frenzied speculation over the height of the building in relation to the length of poor Nigel's final, blood-chilling cry.

Death alone is not the only thing to get listeners and journalists all fired up. One of the programme's most publicised stories was the imprisonment of Susan Carter after she harboured her bad-boy brother Clive Horrobin, on the run for committing a mail van robbery in 1993. Hailed as the Ambridge One by fans (in reference to the miscarriages of justice over the Guildford Four and the Birmingham Six), a fan-led campaign to see her released was soon under way, with Home Secretary Michael Howard joining in the debate. The newspapers lapped up the story with petitions and sensational headlines. Despite public pressure, Susan remained in prison from 23 December 1993 until 31 March. Jenny Webb, the fan who kicked off the campaign by producing posters exclaiming 'Free the Ambridge One!', wanted to draw attention to the fact many women are imprisoned unfairly or too severely for their crimes, leaving families in tatters and children motherless.

Most recently, the programme has been in the news because of its dramatic storylines. More than one newspaper called for 'less excitement' in Ambridge, and A. N. Wilson, writing in *The Daily Telegraph*, said that *Archers* addicts like himself were 'clinging to our seats for dear life' as the quiet Ambridge bus we were on 'seemed to have been taken over by a demon boy-racer, and we were taking dangerous bends on two wheels'. The floods of 2015 were also newsworthy, with some commentators praising the plot for reflecting the reality of flood-hit communities around the country. Others commended the Beeb's use of online technology to provide live blogs, minute-to-minute flood updates, interviews with real-life farmers affected by floods, and realistic weather reports. However, the latter was not to everyone's taste, with the *Daily Mail* reporting that some listeners objected to the blurring of boundaries created by the authentic-seeming news reports. 'She loves the fictional programme,' the friend of a listener was quoted in the *Mail* as saying, 'but knows it is not real life.' What does she mean, it's not real?

LISTENER PORTRAIT

When and why did you start listening? I was born in 1950 so I obviously don't remember the beginning but I do remember the fire that killed Phil's wife. I only listened because my father always had it on at breakfast time on Sundays when we were eating our boiled eggs. My mother could not bear the 'grumbling', probably from Tom Forrest and Walter Gabriel, so she decided to have breakfast in bed!

What's your most memorable Ambridge moment? Not sure there is one but I suppose John dying was pretty bad.

Which character would you most like to meet? I have met some of the cast, but I think I admire the character of Jennifer because she seems to have a lot thrown at her from her husband Brian and various children and works her way through it all without getting too upset. She is also such a 'doer' which I like.

Which character drives you crazy? Surely it has to be Lynda Snell but there was, for a short time a character called Darrell who was just dreadful.

The Archers is wonderful because... it has always tried to be a story about country folk and farming tips and this, on the whole, the writers have preserved.

Carrie Pakenham, author

WELCOME TO AMBRIDGE: WOODBINE COTTAGE

✂ Situated next door to The Bull and opposite the village green, Woodbine was once a tied property owned by Brookfield Farm.

✂ Mabel and Ned Larkin were the Archers' first tenants at Woodbine Cottage, although Ned died shortly after moving in in 1967.

✂ The cottage was bought by Christine Barford and her husband George after their previous home was petrol-bombed by arsonist Clive Horrobin.

✂ Bert and Freda Fry used to live here, but relocated to Brookfield Bungalow when a lorry skidded off the road, destroying part of the cottage.

✂ Next door to Woodbine is Jim Lloyd's home Greenacres. It was built on the site of the Old Police House, which was destroyed in an arson attack. Both Woodbine and Greenacres were damaged by the floods. To add insult to injury, Christine discovered in May 2015 that her house, which had been left empty to dry out, had been burgled.

QUIZ NIGHT AT THE BULL

DEPARTURES AND DEPARTED

1. What object was Arthur Tovey holding that touched a power cable, causing his death in 1976?

2. Whose car was Janet Tregorran in when she died?

3. Christine's first husband, Paul Johnson, died in a car crash in which country?

4. Polly Perks was killed when a tanker skidded into her car – what was in the tanker?

5. Which gamekeeper shot himself in the shepherd's hut in the woods in 2004?

6. How many weeks were there between the deaths of Julia Pargetter and Betty Tucker?

7. Who spent their last days at a clinic in Scotland due to liver failure and passed away in 1972?

8. Who were the two people to find George Barford just in time when he had taken an overdose in 1974?

9. Who died after a family tea party at Glebe Cottage asleep in her chair in 1980?

10. Ralph Bellamy died after suffering a second heart attack in 1980 and had a memorial service in Ambridge, but where was his funeral held?

11. Ivy Horrobin and Freda Fry died from similar causes: what?

12. Bunty and Reg Hebden both died in which year?

ARCHERS EXTRA

Not getting enough from your weekly *Archers* doses? Take a look at some of these websites, books and audio filled with even more wonderful *Archers* information.

WEBSITES

THE BBC ARCHERS HOME PAGE
bbc.co.uk/thearchers
The official site for the programme, previously known as 'Mustardland' due to its slightly garish colour scheme, with family trees, character profiles, blog, and a timeline of key events in the series.

MUSTARDLAND(S)
paranormal.org.uk/mustardland/index.php
mustardland.boards.net
When the message boards were closed on the BBC website, fans took themselves off to two separate mustard-coloured worlds. Both offer busy forums with feverish discussions of the happenings in Borsetshire.

THE ARCHERS ANARCHISTS
archersanarchists.com
The @rchers @narchists know the real truth behind *The Archers*: it's not a serial drama, as so many of us believe, but a fly-on-the-wall documentary about 'a village inhabited by social misfits, murderers and nauseatingly cosy people'. This site is cynical, twisted and very, very funny.

BORSETSHIRE FAMILIES
squiresfamily.me.uk/archers/borsetshire/
A clickable database showing relationships between Ambridge residents past and present. Although it hasn't been updated recently, it is nonetheless a useful guide for the Ambridge newbie.

THE ARCHERS PLOT SUMMARIES
lowfield.co.uk/archers/
Short summaries of life in Ambridge in a particular year, month or episode. The tagline is 'a line a day'. This site is very useful for those little details you have forgotten, and goes back to 1996.

THE HA ARCHERS
haharchers.blogspot.co.uk
Dishing up a lengthy weekly summary since 2010.

PONDERING THE ARCHERS
ponderingthearchers.blogspot.co.uk
In its author's words, this blog is an 'unofficial meander through every episode of *The Archers*' from January 2010 to October 2013, with key quotes and commentary.

THE ARCHERS ADDICTS
facebook.com/pages/Archers-Addicts/43671191219
The official *Archers* fan club has closed its website, but still has a presence on Facebook and Twitter.

ARCHERS APPRECIATION
facebook.com/groups/2215391357/
A busy Facebook group with over 6,000 members. They follow just one rule – thou shalt not be mean about real-life people – which means this funny, rude site is no place for the faint-hearted. Language is not moderated and members regularly 'flounce off' in a huff.

TWITTER

THE ARCHERS
@BBCTheArchers
The official *Archers* Twitter feed has more than 30,000 followers but often finds time to reply to tweeters.

AMBRIDGE SYNTHETICS
@ThePlarchers
The people behind this account spend the Sunday omnibus tweeting pictures of Playmobil figures enacting key *Archers* action. Bizarre, but very funny.

ARCHERS ADDICTS
@ArchersAddicts
Twitter feed of the popular Facebook site.

Most of the characters on *The Archers* have their own Twitter accounts, including @eddie_grundy, @HenryArcher2011 and @LyndaSnell.

BOOKS

THE ARCHERS ARCHIVES
Simon Frith and Chris Arnot
Looking back over 60 years of the programme, scriptwriter Frith and journalist Arnot relive some of the programme's defining moments, with behind-the-scenes exclusives and cast interviews.

WHO'S WHO IN THE ARCHERS 2012
Graham Harvey
The BBC's A–Z round-up of Ambridge's residents is a couple of

years out of date, but is nevertheless packed with information to delight current listeners: a wonderful refresher for an *Archers* fan and a great character introduction for any new listener.

JENNIFER ALDRIDGE'S ARCHERS' COOKBOOK
Angela Piper
With over 150 recipes this season-by-season tour of all of Ambridge's kitchens – from Jennifer's perspective – means you can make Lilian's rich tiramisu without having to pop round for tips.

BRIAN AND ME: LIFE ON – AND OFF – THE ARCHERS
Charles Collingwood
Everything you've ever wanted to know about the charming Brian – and the man who brings him to life.

THE ROAD TO AMBRIDGE: MY LIFE, PEGGY & THE ARCHERS
June Spencer
June is now the only original cast member left in *The Archers*, having played Peggy in the pilot episode. She's been in showbiz since she was twelve, and in this memoir she writes about her long, interesting life, both inside and outside Borsetshire.

THE ARCHERS MISCELLANY
Joanna Toye
Full of delightful titbits from the lives of Ambridge's finest, this little compendium will have you reminiscing about episodes gone by and learning some things you probably never knew about those country folk.

LIFE, LOVE AND THE ARCHERS
Wendy Cope
Actually there's not a huge amount about *The Archers* in this collection of essays, but it's still a great read.

AUDIO AND PODCASTS

THE BEST OF VINTAGE ARCHERS
Relive some of the programme's classic moments with this collection of clips from vintage *Archers* storylines.

AMBRIDGE AFFAIRS: LOVE TRIANGLES
Experience the drama all over again with these collections of episodes featuring Sid Perks's steamy affair and subsequent marriage to Jolene, and Emma Carter's turmoil over the two Grundy brothers.

AMBRIDGE AFFAIRS: HEARTACHE AT HOME FARM
The defining moment of the Aldridges' marriage – Brian's relationship with Siobhan Hathaway – can be unravelled in its entirety with this collection of adulterous episodes.

DUM TEE DUM PODCAST
dumteedum.com
A weekly podcast about *The Archers*, produced by *Archers* fans. It comes out every Monday and you can listen on the site or via iTunes. They also sell interesting merchandise, such as a t-shirt with the slogan 'Hello, you two!'

QUIZ NIGHT AT THE BULL: THE ANSWERS

WHAT'S ON IN AMBRIDGE?

1. Apple Day; 2. Lakey Hill; 3. Harvest Supper; 4. Basil; 5. 1940s; 6. Harry Potter; 7. Reverend Alan Franks; 8. The Flower and Produce Show; 9. Ellen Padbury; 10. India; 11. A Royal Oak sapling; 12. Someone let the bullocks out.

BITES AND PIECES

1. Thursday; 2. Robin Stokes's; 3. January; 4. Marjorie Antrobus; 5. Joe Grundy; 6. Pink Lady®; 7. David Archer; 8. Grey squirrels; 9. Jennifer Aldridge; 10. Meyruelle; 11. Some of his book collection, and £50,000; 12. Phil Archer.

CHARMED CHILDHOODS

1. Prison; 2. Bookcase; 3. Fish; 4. Kate Aldridge; 5. Lakey Hill; 6. Tom; 7. Daniel Mark Archer Hebden Lloyd; 8. Fourteen; 9. Superman; 10. Sharon Richards; 11. A service at St Stephen's Church; 12. A garden statue of a dog, from Eddie Grundy.

FURRY, FOUR-LEGGED FRIENDS

1. Llamas; 2. Walter Gabriel; 3. Alice's; 4. Tolly (Debbie Aldridge's horse); 5. Eccles; 6. Majorie Antrobus; 7. Grace Archer; 8. Red Knight; 9. Captain; 10. In the garden at Nightingale Farm; 11. Baz; 12. Peggy Archer.

LEAVE IT UP TO FÊTE

1. Jill Archer; 2. Marmaduke; 3. 2004; 4. Mum's Army; 5. Neil Carter; 6. Richard Todd; 7. Gin; 8 Knitting; 9. Christine Barford; 10. Carinthia Hart; 11. Kenton, David and Nigel; 12. Fence posts.

HERE COMES THE BRIDE!

1. Peggy; 2. Will Grundy, at Emma and Ed's wedding; 3. Phil Archer and Grace Fairbrother; 4. Jack Archer; 5. Phil Archer; 6. Christine Archer, on her marriage to George Barford; 7. Adam; 8. Grey Gables; 9. John Tregorran; 10. Shula and Mark's; 11. Emma Grundy; 12. Helen.

DOCTOR, DOCTOR!

1. The Netherlands; 2. A patch on her lung; 3. Peggy; 4. John Tregorran; 5. Lilian; 6. Adam; 7. Lasagne; 8. Lynda; 9. Collarbone; 10. Leukaemia; 11. Milly Robson; 12. He was in a car accident.

LONG ARM OF THE LAW

1. Twelve years; 2. Fraud; 3. Susan Carter. She was jailed for harbouring her fugitive brother, Clive Horrobin; 4. Nelson Gabriel; 5. Jazzer; 6. He was selling cannabis; 7. She lied and said that the saboteur started the fight, when she knew that Rob had started it; 8. They destroyed a field of GM crops; 9. He was a policeman; 10. Kathy, during her marriage to Sid; 11. His niece, Emma Carter; 12. Dog fights.

BULLSEYES, BALLS AND WICKETS

1. 1983; 2. Neil Carter; 3. Green and white; 4. Mark Hebden;
5. John Archer, Tom Archer, Christopher Carter and Rob
Titchener; 6. Mrs Perkins's; 7. Sid Perks; 8. Darts; 9. Jack Woolley;
10. Mrs Antrobus; 11. Iftikar ('Ifty') Shah; 12. Brenda Tucker.

WHAT'S FOR DINNER?

1. Jelly; 2. Phil Archer; 3. Balti Triangle; 4. Chutney; 5. Soup;
6. Elizabeth; 7. Rheumatics; 8. Simnel cake; 9. Pip Archer;
10. Phil and Jill Archer's; 11. A whole salmon; 12. Went to get
some more food at The Bull.

LOVE IS IN THE AIR!

1. Prince Andrew and Sarah Ferguson; 2. Brian Aldridge;
3. Stapler; 4. An eternity ring; 5. Nigel Pargetter; 6. A bird book;
7. *The Cherry Orchard*; 8. Joe Grundy; 9. Shula Hebden Lloyd;
10. Elizabeth Archer; 11. Miami; 12. Central Park in New York.

FIELDS AND FARMERS

1. Shorthorns; 2. Brian Aldridge; 3. A market garden; 4. Brookfield
Farm; 5. Sterling Gold; 6. Bellamy Estate; 7. Myxomatosis;
8. Grange Farm; 9. Boxer; 10. Milk quotas; 11. The dairy herd;
12. Adam Macy.

FARMING FASHIONS

1. A fox-fur coat; 2. Elizabeth Pargetter and Sophie Barlow;
3. Eddie Grundy; 4. Jeans; 5. Nigel Pargetter; 6. Kenton Archer;
7. Underwoods; 8. A Harris tweed jacket; 9. Hats; 10. Pink;
11. Her stage costumes; 12. A tiger onesie.

OUT OF TOWN

1. Birmingham New Street; 2. Loxley Barrett; 3. Women's shoes;
4. Felpersham; 5. The King's Head; 6. Video shop; 7. Tapas;
8. A centre for children with special needs; 9. Germany;
10. Sixteen; 11. Darrington; 12. Hollerton Junction.

WISH YOU WERE HERE!

1. Spain; 2. Jolene; 3. The Italian Riviera; 4. Christine Archer;
5. Burglary; 6. Nigel and Elizabeth Pargetter; 7. The Seychelles;
8. Phil and Jill Archer; 9. Her cashmere cardigan; 10. Carol Grey;
11. Las Vegas; 12. Costa Rica.

NEW LIFE, NEW STRIFE

1. William; 2. France; 3. Kate Aldridge; 4. Indian; 5. Brian Aldridge;
6. Jaundice; 7. David Archer; 8. Hip; 9. Christopher Carter;
10. Meriel; 11. Ethan; 12. Bethany Tucker.

COMPETITIONS, CURTSEYS AND CURTAIN-UPS

1. Giant car boot sale; 2. *Jack and the Beanstalk*; 3. The Dirty Duck; 4. Phil Archer; 5. Christopher Carter; 6. 'The Brilliant and The Dark'; 7. Pip Archer; 8. Fake blood; 9. Mike and Betty Tucker; 10. Fallon Rogers; 11. Joe Grundy; 12. Edith the maid.

O COME, ALL YE FAITHFUL

1. 1928; 2. John Ridley; 3. Vet; 4. Janet Fisher; 5. London; 6. Shula Hebden Lloyd; 7. Grace Archer; 8. Christine Archer and George Barford; 9. Kenya; 10. Clock weights; 11. Darrell Makepeace; 12. Penny Hassett, Edgeley and Darrington.

DOWN ON THE FARM

1. Bridge Farm; 2. Hereford beef; 3. Ed Grundy; 4. 100 acres; 5. Home Farm; 6. Queencups; 7. The chickens; 8 .The Grundys; 9. Maize; 10. 1958; 11. Berrow Farm; 12. At Young Farmers.

AMBRIDGE EXTRA

1. Five; 2. Brenda Tucker; 3. A pair of Y-fronts (new and still in the pack, thankfully); 4. She brokered a loan from her housemate Chaz; 5. That while at school she attacked a classmate with a knife; 6. Erin, Daniel's sort-of girlfriend; 7. Clive Horrobin; 8. Lance; 9. Mandisa; 10. Edinburgh; 11. Stealing money from the collection plate; 12. He was murdered.

EVENTS OF THE YEAR

1. Blue; 2. Florrie Hoskins's; 3. 1995; 4. Phil Archer; 5. Tony; 6. Pru Forrest; 7. A French maid's outfit; 8. Alcohol; 9. Doris Archer; 10. Quaintance Smith; 11. A Father's Day card she'd bought for Brian; 12. Sid Perks.

DEPARTURES AND DEPARTED

1. Aluminium ladder; 2. Charles Grenville's; 3. Germany; 4. Milk; 5. Greg Turner; 6. Six; 7. Jack Archer; 8. Tom and Pru Forrest; 9. Doris Archer; 10. Guernsey; 11. Heart failure following pneumonia; 12. 2013.

FOREWORD BY
PIPPA GREENWOOD

FOR THE LOVE OF
RADIO 4

AN UNOFFICIAL
COMPANION

CAROLINE HODGSON

FOR THE LOVE OF RADIO 4

Caroline Hodgson

ISBN: 978-1-84953-642-4

Hardback

£9.99

From *Farming Today* at sunrise to the gentle strains of 'Sailing By' and the Shipping Forecast long after midnight, Radio 4 provides the soundtrack to life for millions of Britons. In *For the Love of Radio 4*, Caroline Hodgson celebrates all that's best about the nation's favourite spoken-word station, taking us on a tour through its history, its key personalities and programmes, and countless memorable moments from the archives.

'I found the book to be full of fascinating detail. It is clearly a labour of love, perfectly designed for Radio 4 lovers.'

Simon Brett

'If you love Radio 4 it's impossible to turn it off. If you read this book it's impossible to put down.'

Charles Collingwood

A CELEBRATION OF THE
WORLD'S FINEST MUSIC

FOR THE LOVE OF
CLASSICAL
MUSIC

A COMPANION

CAROLINE HIGH

FOR THE LOVE OF CLASSICAL MUSIC

Caroline High

ISBN: 978-1-84953-732-2

Hardback

£9.99

From Bach to Beethoven, Vivaldi to Vaughan Williams, the world of classical music has something to enchant every listener. Whether you're an armchair connoisseur, a regular concert-goer or an ardent musician, *For the Love of Classical Music* will take you on a tour encompassing landmark pieces and performances, key artists and composers, and surprising facts about the world's most beautiful music.

The
Countryside
Year

Steve Barnett

THE COUNTRYSIDE YEAR

Steve Barnett

ISBN: 978-1-84953-683-7

Hardback

£9.99

This charming and practical handbook is bursting with tips, facts and folklore to guide you through the countryside year. Find out how to identify birds by sight or song, spot animal tracks, name wild flowers, butterflies, insects and trees, and forage for natural foods throughout the seasons.

With handy diary pages for making your own notes each month as you explore the hills, forests and fields, this is a must-have for any lover of the great outdoors.

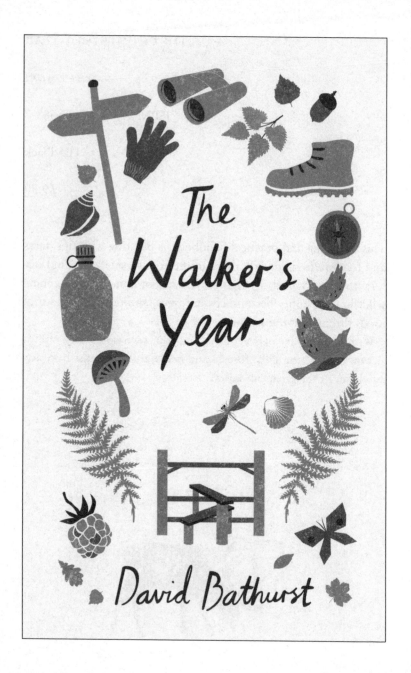

The Walker's Year

David Bathurst

THE WALKER'S YEAR

David Bathurst

ISBN: 978-1-84953-696-7

Hardback

£9.99

This charming and practical handbook is bursting with tips, facts
and folklore to guide those who love to roam through the natural
rhythms and seasons of the year. Find out how to identify flora by
colour and shape, discover routes of outstanding natural beauty
and learn about the diverse wildlife that can be found across
Britain.

With useful notes pages for documenting your exploration of
countryside, shore, cliffs and forests, this is a must-have for any
lover of the great outdoors!

If you're interested in finding out more about our books, find us on Facebook at **Summersdale Publishers** and follow us on Twitter at **@Summersdale**.

www.summersdale.com